WHAT EVERY CHRISTIAN SHOULD KNOW ABOUT ISLAM

RUQAIYYAH WARIS MAQSOOD

THE ISLAMIC FOUNDATION

Dedicatory Verses

The only true religion in the sight of God is a human's self-surrender to Him.

(Surah 3:19)

If anyone goes in search of a religion other than self-surrender to God, it will never be accepted by Him, and in the life to come, he/she will be among the lost.

(Surah 3:85)

Published by
THE ISLAMIC FOUNDATION,
Markfield Conference Centre,
Ratby Lane, Markfield,
Leicester LE67 9SY, United Kingdom
Tel: (01530) 244944/5, Fax: (01530) 244946
E-mail: i.foundation@islamic-foundation.org.uk
Web site: http://www.islamic-foundation.org.uk

QURAN HOUSE, P.O. Box 30611, Nairobi, Kenya

P.M.B. 3193, Kano, Nigeria

ISBN 0 86037 375 4 (PB)

Typeset by: N.A. Qaddoura
Cover design: Imtiaze A. Manjra

Contents

Section One – The Religious Beliefs of Islam Explained 1

Muslims are not the enemy – the Crusades are over! 1
The statement of faith 6
Belief in God, His Unity – *Tawhid* 6
How can we know about the 'nature' of God? 14
Belief in the Angels 16
Belief in the Books 20
Belief in the Messengers 23
Are Muslims fatalists? If God knows everything in advance surely it must all be pre-determined? 24
Belief in the Life to Come 27
Belief in Judgement, Heaven and Hell 29
What do Muslims mean by *dhikr*, or 'Remembering' Allah? 35
Do we stay married in Heaven? What happens in cases of polygamy, or where people have married more than once because of death or divorce? 38

Section Two - The Religious Duties of Islam Explained 43

What is meant by the phrase 'the pillars of Islam'? What are these pillars? 43
What is special, or different, about Muslim prayer? 43
Do Muslims have any Clergy? 47
What is the 'religious tax'? Is it the same as the Jewish tithe, or the Christian covenant subscription? 49
What is meant by fasting? 50
What is meant by *Hajj*? 52
What is that big black cube-shaped building? 55

Section Three - Miscellaneous Questions 59

Is Islam compatible with modern science? 59
What is the difference between Sunni and Shi'ite Islam? 60
Are Muslims always fighting? 62
Are Muslims extremists? 64
Is it true that Muslim women cannot choose their own husbands? 66
How do Muslims Treat Young Children? 67
Do Muslims force girls into marrying too soon? 69
What do Muslims think about 'female circumcision'? 71
Can a Muslim marry more than one wife? 72
Can a Muslim man divorce his wife without legal proceedings? 75
Do divorced Muslim men kidnap their children and take them away? 76
Do Muslim men regard women as inferior? 77

Are Muslim men allowed to beat their wives? 78
Why are so many Muslims called Abdul? Or Ben? Or Hajji? Or Al? 80
Can Muslims who live in the UK join in with Christmas celebrations? 81
Why cannot Muslims eat pork? 83
What is halal slaughter? 84
Why do Muslims think that all the normal world wide banking systems are wrong? 86
Were the Savage Mongol Armies Muslim? 87
What about Israel and the PLO? 88
Are Muslims trying to take over the world? 90

SECTION FOUR - CHRISTIANITY AND ISLAM 97

What changes of belief would Christians have to make if they accepted Islam? 97
There is only One True God. Jehovah (Yahweh), Our Father in Heaven, and Allah are one and the same God 102
If Jews, Christians and Muslims really do all worship the same God, why cannot they just get together and become one faith? 106
How then do Muslims account for the differences between Jew, Christian and Muslim? 110
What about all the Christian Unitarians who do not believe in a Holy Trinity? 111
Why is the Qur'an regarded as such a holy text? 113
Is it true that Muslims believe that Jesus and the Jewish prophets were Muslim too? 115
Is it true that Muslims believe that the Prophet Muhammad was greater than Jesus 116

What do Muslims believe about the Way to God? 118
How do Muslims differ from Chrisians in their beliefs about Jesus? 119
Is there any evidence in the Chrisian holy books that the Muslim position concerning Jesus could possibly be right? 121
If Christian believe that 'no person can come to the Father but by Me (Jesus)', then surely Muslims and Christians can never be reconciled? 123
What do Muslims teach about personal salvation? 124
What does Islam teach about forgiveness? 127
What do Muslims think Jesus taught about personal salvation? 129
If Muhammad was really a genuine prophet, why was he not foretold in the Bible as Jesus was? 131
If Muslims are supposed to accept that all Jewish prophets were genuine, why do they not have the same reverence for the Old Testament that Jews and Christians have? 134
Do Muslims believe in miracles? 139
My mother's question - Why did my daughter, who I have always believed to be intelligent and in her right mind, choose to become one of these Muslims? 140

INDEX 147

SECTION ONE

The Religious Beliefs of Islam Explained

Muslims are not the enemy – the Crusades are over!

There are around two million Muslims in the UK, and Islam is spreading rapidly in Europe and the Western world. In Britain today there are certainly more practising Muslims than practising Anglicans. Yet this disparity is not the result of a massive influx of immigrants, or the tendency of immigrant people to produce large families. Moreover, it has occurred despite the bad publicity earned by various Islamic terrorists and extremists.

There has been a sudden flowering of accurate and unbiased literature on Islam. The world is shrinking; it is no longer possible to remain proud of one's ignorance. Most UK schools now feature a well-planned introduction to Islam (along with other world faiths) on their syllabus enabling young people to improve their knowledge and understanding of the world's religions. One perhaps unexpected result of this process is that when the students become adults they will be able to make informed choices regarding their religion, and no longer automatically choose the faith of their own families.

In earlier days, no world religions other than Christianity were offered in the classroom. Comparative religion was grudgingly squeezed in, so long as the teacher made it clear that the other faith being introduced was not only inferior to Christianity but also wrong and even laughable, ignorant or evil. Nowadays, every effort is made to impart knowledge accurately, and not to the detriment of other faiths. So, inevitably, after being presented with a range of possibilities, and having grown up alongside friends of these other faiths, young people will begin to make independent choices.

However, a common concern among Muslim parents in the UK, is that their teenage children will be seduced by the behaviour of their non-Muslim counterparts who drink, take drugs, enjoy sexual freedom, and regard sexual aberrations as normal. What the Muslim population may perhaps not have realised is that many thousands of non-Muslim youngsters being educated in the same State schools now have the opportunity to choose another route. They may examine the various merits of the faiths taught to them, and as a result may choose to leave *their* own culture to become Muslim. The seeds are rapidly being sown. Who knows what harvest may be gleaned in the future!

A healthy, growing faith only grows because of the appeal and reasonableness of that faith. Thinking persons who take the trouble to explore the beliefs of Islam soon realise that they are not monstrous. They have nothing to do with the terrorism that offends everyone – Muslim as much as non-Muslim. They ring true, are in keeping with natural law and reason, and give acceptable answers to the challenges of life.

Let us ignore the Muslim hotheads, who are about as representative of real Islam as IRA terrorists are of the Roman Catholic Church; let us ignore the various corrupt and cruel leaders of certain Muslim countries, who are about as representative of the real Islam as the Borgia Popes or the zealous chiefs of the Inquisition were of true Christianity; let us ignore the 'Islamic' nationalistic and political issues – which may well be noble and justified, but are religious only in the sense that an escape is sought from injustice and persecution.

Let us not make the common mistake of judging the tenets of any religion by the ignorance or misbehaviour of many of its less noble adherents.

Muslims do not consider themselves to be the enemies of Christians and Jews as such. Muslims are actually called upon to *accept* the genuine revealed teachings, not only of Jesus, who was himself a Jew, but also of the earlier prophets, including Abraham, Moses, Solomon, Amos, Hosea, Isaiah, Jeremiah, Ezekiel and John the Baptist.

People these days are not usually frightened of or antagonistic towards Jews, Hindus or Buddhists. There are many reasons why Islam is regarded by so many westerners as 'the enemy'. One is that Muslims seem to 'look down their noses' at everyone else. Some are *so* ostentatiously religious that their behaviour antagonises the 'British spirit' of modesty and under-statement. Those who cannot follow the path of puritanism and abstinence resent the notion that they are inferior to those who can. Moreover, there is little to admire in the conduct of many so-called Islamic leaders in today's world. Indeed, there is considerable evidence that once in power these regimes somehow lose sight of the purity, gentleness, compassion and tolerance of Islam, and instead become repressive to dissenters – especially women – and their leaders become corrupt and hypocritical. Islam is also regarded by Christians as a direct challenge to the theology of Christianity.

The fears are genuine enough. It is patently not sufficient for Muslim scholars to point out repeatedly that oppressive and abusive Islamists are not true Muslims; those Islamists doggedly maintain their total allegiance to Islam, and accuse dissenting Muslims of being either decadent, ignorant, or 'half-baked'.

Until Muslims are able to communicate the genuine teachings of Islam, elevate truly noble and pious persons to positions of leadership, and accept that a difference exists between a political leader and a scholar or religious 'saint' (a term not actually favoured in Islam), the fears remain valid. It is up to Muslims to put their own house in order, as quickly as possible.

The specifically Christian fear is also reasonable. Those growing up in the Christian faith, loving and serving God to the best of their ability, and striving to lead unselfish, caring and compassionate lives, feel that the mainstay of their faith is love for the Lord Jesus Christ. One's depth as a true Christian can often be tested against the lengths one is prepared to go in order to sacrifice one's self to the will of God as revealed by Jesus.

It is the hardest thing in the world, and seems so unreasonable and such a betrayal, for a Christian to consider that, whereas belief in God is absolutely required, it is not only mistaken but *wrong* to believe that Jesus was His Son, in that special Trinitarian sense. It is so automatic to end one's prayers with the phrases 'in Jesus' name', or 'through Jesus Christ our Lord'. Since childhood Christians have celebrated, with rituals enhanced by emotion, God being born as a helpless baby in the Bethlehem stable at Christmas, the sacrificial death of Jesus on the cross and his subsequent resurrection to glory at Easter – the two supreme demonstrations of God's amazing love for humanity. The more humble, adoring and fervent the Christian in response to this incredible love (quite unearned by us, but the gift of God's grace), the nearer to God, or so Christians are taught to believe. It takes enormous moral courage to stand back from this viewpoint and reconsider the grounds of one's faith.

The statement of faith

The Muslim statement of faith is very simple:

> *'La ilaha ilallah wa Muhammad ur-rasul ullah'.*

'There is no God but Allah (the One), and Muhammad is the prophet of Allah.'

A longer statement is known as the *Iman al-Mufassal*, or the 'Faith in detail'. This lists seven specific things:

> *'I believe in Allah, in His angels, in His Revealed books; in all of His prophets; in the Day of Judgement; in that everything – both good and evil – comes from Him; and in life after death.'*

All these beliefs are supported by Biblical texts and also by Jewish texts, such as the Talmud and Mishnah.

Belief in God, His unity – *Tawhid*

This is the most basic and fundamental of beliefs. It can be approached from two main question-points; firstly, does God exist at all, or is the whole notion nonsense; and secondly, if there is such a concept as 'divinity', how many divine beings are there? Is there only one – or are there two opposing equal forces, like light/darkness, or good/evil, – or are there a whole order of divine beings, perhaps running into millions?

Each of these points of view has had its supporters throughout history. One thing is quite certain; the belief in some Divine Entity has existed as long as we have proof of human existence. Various burial customs strongly suggest a belief in life after death. But is it all just wishful thinking?

The last century saw an enormous shift in the way people in the west have looked at 'life, the universe, and everything'. It has not been quite the same in the eastern world, and this is usually attributed to the fact that the industrial revolution and the march of scientific materialism 'progressed' in the west earlier than it did in the east; the supposition is that the east will soon go the same way. In the West, God is no longer the central topic of conversation around the table, in the home, at work, even, sometimes, at the place of worship, as He still is in a Muslim home.

Much of the rejection of the notion that God is necessary to one's life goes back to the fierce controversies of the nineteenth century, the feelings of liberation from the pompous authority of the Church, and the ridiculous notion that salvation was only possible through blind faith. The 'Church' had shown itself as condoning corruption in high places,[1] sheltering clergymen whose notion of how God wanted them to save souls was horrendous,[2] and involved slaughtering those who did not believe what *they* themselves believed, or wished to read the Bible in their own languages. The history of the great martyrs of the Church, those who would rather die than compromise their principles, and those who gave up their lives entirely to the service of suffering humanity, is largely a history of people resisting the powers-that-be, many of whom formed the Church hierarchy. Such abuse has made people highly suspicious and resentful of hypocrisy in high places, a feeling which remains very strong today.[3]

Then came the march of scriptural criticism. People made a deep study of the background and sources of the Biblical texts, and challenged the notion that they were inspired, word for word. Also, the march of science, discovered more and more about the universe, filling the gaps in human knowledge. It became fashionable to call God the 'God of the gaps' because His sphere of activity and relevance was being more and more pushed back into those gaps in our knowledge which, it was hoped (by atheists), would all be filled in as soon as possible by scientific discovery – the most significant being the origin of the universe, the origin of life, the origin of sexual difference and reproduction as opposed to cells endlessly replicating identically, the origin of the soul, and the origin of the idea of God.

This is one side of the picture. On the other side can be found the devout and politically innocent believers to whom all the aforementioned matter little – they just busy themselves with their worship, as they have always done.

The fact remains that the existence of God cannot yet be scientifically proved, and probably never will be. Perhaps it is not intended to be. However, there is an enormous amount of circumstantial evidence and countless pages of theological argument to consider. The major arguments usually put forward are these:

> *First Cause* – that unless something is caused it does not exist. Everything in our universe is caused. Something therefore must have caused it. Whatever that cause was, that we may call God, even if we have no idea of what God is.[4]
>
> *First Movement* – that unless something is moved by forces acting upon it, it does not move. Everything in the universe is in motion. Whatever it was that activated the whole lot, that we may call God.[5]
>
> *Contingency* – the reverse of the First Cause argument. If a thing might not have existed, it is called *contingent*. You are a contingent being because you might never have existed.[6] Is it possible that our entire solar system might not have existed? Of course. It is therefore contingent. It must exist for a *reason,* a cause. Is it possible that the entire cosmos with all its universes might never have existed? We suppose

so – therefore the whole lot is contingent. Thus, there must have been something which caused it all to be, and that we call God.[7]

Necessary Being – this is also called the *Ontological argument* because it involves a logical play on words. God must be 'necessary' because a scale of values exists. Some things are bad, some are better, some are much better, and at the top there is that which is best. Can there be two 'bests'? No, not by definition of what we mean by best. That which is at the top of our values we may call God. And He must exist because that which does not exist cannot be the best; if it doesn't exist it cannot be regarded as supremely *anything.*[8] Therefore if there is a supreme of the scale of values, it, or He, must exist.

Design – this is also called the *Teleological argument* because it looks forward to an end, aim or goal. The universe in every aspect of its laws and their physical manifestations shows order and pattern – in other words, design. They do not appear to have come about by accident. If it is true that things have evolved, they have evolved to a pattern, and seem to be moving towards an ultimate goal, even if we do not know what that goal is.[9]

These five arguments are known as the Classical Arguments, and ever since they were first propounded in the Middle Ages by St. Thomas

Aquinas (for the Christians) and Ibn al-Arabi (for the Muslims), they have raged on, with few, if any, modifications.

There are two other important arguments for the existence of God. Firstly, that 'He' as a concept has entered human consciousness at all. Why should such a concept ever have arisen if there has never been such an Entity? Is it possible to conceive of something which does not exist and has never been part of human experience? Yes, some answer. We are able to imagine all sorts of monsters that do not and never have existed. Every fan of horror films can easily imagine Monsters from the Black Lagoon. They point out that all these creations were modelled on real-life creatures,- such as dinosaurs.

The last important argument concerns those who have religious experiences, who feel aware of God's presence, who perhaps have visions, see angels, have moments of mystical awareness, or experienced flashes of insight into the future? Where could all these experiences come from, if not from God?

Unfortunately, it has to be admitted that mental institutions contain a high proportion of such people. 'The Yorkshire Ripper' heard the 'voice of God' exhorting him to cut the throats of prostitutes. Thus the atheist rests his/her case. It is always unsafe to base beliefs on emotions, mystical experiences or states of altered consciousness – one of the major criticisms of such contemporary religious manifestations as the 'Toronto blessing', emotional soul-singing, speaking in tongues, New Age Christianity, or the trance-states induced by Sufi *dhikr*.

One of the ways that chants, incantations, and emotionalism work is to 'numb' the mind in order to deliberately alter its state of consciousness and promote 'alpha' states. Thus are generated visions and impulses that are visual images, intuitions and feelings. The person may enjoy a dramatic sense of well-being, an 'openness to God' or a sense of 'being at one with God', or 'at one with nature' or the universe – but this is deceptive. Altered mind states make us open to things other than God, including evil matters and entities that come clothed in beautiful disguises.

When we cut to the bottom line, no matter how brilliant our brains, or how sensitive our insights and intuitions – it still comes down to a matter of faith, in the sense of accepting things that apparently cannot be proved.

When it comes to *what* believers believe about their God or gods, these are hardly matters that can be forced on a person. People believe what it seems right to them to believe. They follow their own sense of logic and their own conscience. They use such mental equipment as they have and can do no more. Some, of course, settle for a slavish acceptance of what others, probably those in authority, tell them to believe.

Therefore, you are free to examine all the world's faiths with your own brains. Muslims believe very strongly that 'truth stands clear from error' (Surah 2:256), that God does exist, and that there is only one Supreme Being, the Almighty (or Allah – the translation into Arabic of 'almighty'). They believe that all things, good and evil, must of necessity have their origin in Him, and that there must be a reason why the universe is as it is, and why people are as they are, and why the tests in their lives come along as they do. They do not choose between a universe initiated by a Big Bang or no universe at all, but a universe begun by a Big Bang or any other origin after *with* God, or one without Him. The actual arguments regarding the origin of the universe or the theory of evolution are irrelevant to the existence of God. Muslims may take them or leave them, and generally consider it wiser to adopt a 'wait and see' attitude to the claims of science. They see the evidence of cause and design in everything and are aware that everything is contingent and their own lives or fortunes, could be changed in a flash. They believe humans should be humble and be aware that however much they know, there are millions of things that they do not know.

They will never accept that God has a partner, or sharer, or would ever intermingle His 'substance' in the world of physical matter by engendering half-human offspring. They do not believe that any other thing could possibly have power over God – whether a sacrifice, the pleas of the devout, a rival spirit entity, or a lucky charm! No-one can possibly 'know better' than God, or have more compassion than God.[10] Muslims do not believe that any other mind has the right to pass ultimate judgement, for they do not have the background knowledge that God has. We have no right to assume that such-and-such a person is evil, or a saint. How do we know?

All these things are part of what a Muslim calls *tawhid*, the One-ness of God. Thoughts about tawhid are continued in the next section.

How can we know about the 'nature' of God?

We can only have a very limited awareness of it. Muslims are extremely careful never to associate any image or thing with God. 'Nothing is like unto Him' (Surah 42:11). *Nothing* in the whole of creation is Allah, or partakes of Allah, or is in any way associated with Allah. God is inexpressible. It is even misleading to call God 'Him', which implies sexuality.

All the references that seem to suggest that God has a physical body, with mouth, tongue, eyes and ears, should be interpreted symbolically. Did God 'speak' to the Prophets or 'sit' on a throne? Or do these passages mean rather that God's revelation was conveyed to the human mind, and that God has almighty power?

Muslims believe, however, that important clues have been revealed in the 'Beautiful Names' of God – none of which are names as such, but which refer to His *attributes*, and express His lordship of the universe and His providence in it. Since God Himself revealed these names as part of the Qur'an, Muslims can study and use them as true guides to the 'character' and 'personality' of God.

You will often hear Muslims talk about the 100 Beautiful Names, but in fact, if one takes the trouble to count up all the Names mentioned in the Qur'an, the total is more than 100. It is also untrue to claim that there are only 99 names on a chart, since the 100th name is known only to the camel, and that is why it seems to wear a superior smile! I have no idea where that ridiculous piece of nonsense originated – but I suspect British troops in the Middle East in the early years of this century had something to do with it. Any chart, such as the one reproduced here, chooses from the full collection of Beautiful Names available.

Not all of them are comfortable. True, God is *as-Salaam* (the Source of Peace), *al-Wahab* (the Bestower), *al-Basir* (the All-Seeing), *al-Wali* (the Protecting Friend) and *al-Afuw* (the Pardoner); but He is also *al-Muntaqim* (the Avenger), *al-Mani* (the Preventer), *al-Khafid* (the Abaser), *al-Muhsi* (the Reckoner) and *al-Mumit* (the Annihilator).

What is most significant to a Christian is the realisation that at no time in the entire 23 years of the Revelation to Muhammad did God ever refer to Himself as *Father.* This must have been deliberate. A Muslim can certainly call God 'Rabb' or 'Master', but not 'Abb' or 'Father'. One can only guess the reason for the omission of this familiar way of referring to God, the most likely being that it has obvious physical connotations, and can lead people astray. It became a commonplace title for God after the coming of Jesus, and as a result of the success of Trinitarianism, has led to much unprofitable speculation. God is not our Father, except in the symbolic sense, that He is our Creator. Christians may not realise that God was never referred to as Father in the Torah; the first references occur in Isaiah 9:6 and 64:8, Psalm 68:5 and Jeremiah 31:9. Apart from these, the references to God as Father only occur in the New Testament.

Many Muslims make a study of the given Names of God, which form the starting point for their thoughts about God. Many Names are recited as reminders.

Belief in the Angels

Like belief in God, this is another issue on which people have strong views, but where little in the way of proof exists. Belief in angels is another aspect of religion that has been strongly challenged in recent years, although many devotees are totally convinced that they exist, have felt their presence in many situations, and would be quite prepared to swear that these experiences are real.

Some people seem to be much more sensitive to the presence of angels than others, but we should be careful before envying this quality; it may not only depend on personality, or saintliness, but on deception or mental disorder!

Some religious faiths have strong beliefs in angels, but have misleading or misguided opinions about them. Muslims feel that this is particularly true of New Age religion, in which people are urged to seek contact with angels and spirit guides, and to become more spiritual by assisting them in their good works. Granting to angels power of their own to intervene in events and lives is not suggested the Bible or the Qur'an.

To the Muslim there is no doubt that angels exist and pervade the entire universe. They are believed to be a completely different order of creation from human beings, and not just 'dead people' who carry on working and loving their relatives on earth from the world of the 'great beyond'. Souls and/or spirits of humans (or animals) are quite different from angels. The invocation of angels or spirit guides places a person in danger of summoning an evil entity in disguise, and moves them one step further away from trusting in God.

The angels have always been regarded as expressing the will of God. One finds this belief in the earliest strata of the Old Testament. Moreover, that which many Christians would probably regard as the action of the Holy Spirit, Muslims would attribute to the work of angels. Traditionally they have been concerned with delivering God's messages and revelations to humanity, watching over the humans to whom they have been assigned, stirring the consciences of people vulnerable to temptation as a means of preventing a bad act or putting things right. They have alerted people to dangers; they have manifested themselves as a wonderful feeling of peace in the midst of panic and confusion, as grace during times of prayer, as joy at various uplifting moments in human experience, as unseen companions when people are going through the depths of loneliness and depression.

Some people sense that the angels care about them and their lives. Strange coincidences frequently happen that seem too amazing just to be put down to coincidence. Some religious people (I would include myself and my non-Muslim mother in this!) appear to have the ability to send a mental cry for help when they need something, perhaps only a detail of information, and it somehow turns up. Although we must beware of imagining that angels exist to serve us, people in difficulties somehow manage to connect with those who can help them, and it really does feel as if they have been directed there. Sleep on a problem, and the answer – or a sensible course of action – somehow miraculously becomes clear.

However, angels do not as a rule rescue people from their perils and predicaments – unless specifically ordered by God to do so. They may observe, but they do not necessarily intervene. Nor do they respond to human prayers, no matter how desperate, unless ordered by God to do so.

It is not expected that every single person will be aware of angelic activity going on around them, but Muslims accept that they exist and are around us, and feel comfortable with that. They probably could not imagine life without angels. Seeing angels should never be regarded as a reward for a life of merit or piety. Most people who see angels are not being 'saintly' at all – but are in a fix. Those who *do* see an angel almost never see one with wings and brilliant lights; the angel appears usually in human form, does what it has been sent to do (or say what it has been sent to say) and then disappears.[11]

The main beliefs about angels in Islam are that every person is allocated at least two – the recorders, who keep a note of all one's good and bad deeds.[12] The record of good deeds is permanent, but the record of bad deeds is wiped out on repentance. Angels surround people when they are praying and when they are in need or in danger; religious people are often particularly aware of them at the pre-dawn prayer time. There are certain special angels with special functions, such as *Jibril* (Gabriel), the chief messenger of God; *Mikail*, the guardian of holy places; *Azrail*, the angel of death; *Israfil*, who will signal the resurrection at the Day of Judgement; *Munkir* and *Nakir*, the angels who will question the souls of the newly-dead. There are many, many others, and many references to them in the Qur'an and hadiths.

One of the happiest references to angels in the Qur'an is where they are described as descending to the faithful as they pray. They say: 'Do not be afraid, and do not be sad. Understand and believe the good news about the state of Paradise which you have been promised. We are your protecting friends, in the life of this world, and in the next.' (Surah 41:30–32).[13]

Satan, or *Shaytan*, is not thought of in Islam as a fallen angel – a concept which ought to be impossible anyway – but as the chief of another order of beings, the *jinn*. These are frequently regarded as 'evil spirits', but this is incorrect. They *can* be evil, and/or mischievous – but are not necessarily so. Often they live quite happily alongside humans without troubling them. The Qur'an records one occasion when a group of *jinn* listened to the Prophet and accepted Islam. *Shaytan* became the cause of a great deal of evil when God did not 'take his advice' not to create human beings with freewill; he disobeyed God, became jealous, resentful and hostile – but human beings, with the help of God and His angels, do not need to fear either him or his agents, so long as they keep seeking the 'straight path'.[14]

Belief in the Books

The most important holy book to Muslims is obviously the Qur'an. It is worth repeating that this was not written by the Prophet Muhammad as a book, but was a series of messages from God which came to him bit by bit over a period of 23 years. Sometimes he received these revelations frequently, and sometimes there were long gaps between one and the next. They were not revealed as a consecutive narrative, but usually came in response to some particular problem which was taxing either the Prophet or his followers. Some revelations were very long, others very short. The long surahs were not delivered all in one piece, nor necessarily in the order in which they appear now. The order of the Qur'an as we now have it was not arbitrary, but taught to the Prophet in his final year, and that has been the order ever since. It did not begin like that, and the earliest parts of the 'Book' are not the earliest parts to be revealed. The text has no chronological value, but presents the answers to various questions. In a very few places a later revelation revised slightly what had been taught in an earlier one, and in these cases, the later revelation is accepted as the binding one.

It is impossible for other material to have been 'sneaked' into the Qur'an after the Prophet's lifetime, since its accuracy can be vouched for over and over again by the many thousands of Muslims who are *huffaz*, who have learnt the whole lot by heart. Most of the Prophet's companions did this, and the tradition has persisted ever since. The first completed hand-written copy was given into the safe-keeping of the Prophet's wife Hafsah, daughter of Caliph Umar, and can be seen today in Tashkent and Istanbul museums. It has now been photocopied by modern equipment, so the accuracy can always be checked on the internet.

Other books that are considered to be part of God's Revelation to humanity include the works of Musa (Moses), Dawud (David), Sulayman (Solomon), the other Biblical prophets, and the original Injil (from the word Evangel) or Gospel of Jesus – which is not to be identified with the books of the New Testament as we now have them. Muslims respect these texts, but are wary of them, since they cannot know for certain which verses are straight revelations from God and which have been altered in some way by human editors.

However, a Christian could list those things that comprise the various prophets' messages over a period of at least a thousand years, and would no doubt find that they were absolutely consistent – as having come from the One and the Same Divine Source. All those teachings would be perfectly acceptable to Muslims because they are also consistent with the Qur'an, which came from the Same Source.

Anything written by the prophets at God's command was 'inspired' writing. Muslims can accept the Bible as containing the 'inspired word of God', but they cannot accept the notion that all the narrative and editorial work was inspired because God was guiding the human workers on the text. They maintain that what was not specifically said by God was the work of human minds and hands, and all humans are fallible.

However, the Bible is a great miracle in the sense that the entire literature of a people during a period of over a thousand years concerned the same hero – God. So many writers who had probably never read each other's work, all seemed to have been activated by one and the same Source, who may have revealed different things at different times and in different circumstances, but whose message was always consistent.

Belief in the Messengers

Islam teaches that thousands of Messengers were sent to every age and every society. 'There is no people but We have sent them a warner' (Surah 14:4; 25:51; 35:24).

Twenty-five were mentioned by name in the Qur'an, the major prophets being Nuh (Noah), Ibrahim (Abraham), Musa (Moses), Sulayman (Solomon) and Isa (Jesus). Three mentioned in the Qur'an were not mentioned in the Bible – Hud, Salih and Shu'ayb, although some identify the latter with Jethro, the Midianite father-in-law of Moses. The full list of those in the Qur'an who are also named in the Bible is as follows: Adam, Idris (Enoch), Nuh (Noah), Ibrahim (Abraham), Ismail (Ishmael), Ishaq (Isaac), Yaqub (Jacob), Yusuf (Joseph), Ayyub (Job), Musa (Moses), Harun (Aaron), Dhulfikl (Ezekiel), Dawud (David), Sulayman (Solomon), Ilyas (Elijah), Al-Yas'a (Elisha), Yunus

(Jonah), Zakariyyah (Zechariah), Yahya (John the Baptist), and Isa (Jesus). Muhammad was the last prophet in this line. There have been no further prophets since the revelation of the Qur'an.

This list was not intended to be the full list of prophets which, Muslim tradition states, amounted to thousands.

But why did God send prophets anyway? It was because of His justice. Prophets are specially chosen people who are granted the ability to know the will of God and reveal it to humanity. If it is true that after human life ends there will be a time of Judgement, and we will receive either reward for our good lives or punishment for our evil, then if God is fair, He must make it quite clear to people what He regards as good and evil. Otherwise, our ignorance would lead to our downfall, and this would make God extremely *unfair.* God is beyond our ability to know and understand. We cannot know Him, unless He chooses to reveal Himself to us. That is why the prophets were sent – to show us the way. We are not forced to do God's will. It is left to our own choice.

Are Muslims fatalists? If God knows everything in advance surely it must all be pre-determined?

The concept of *al-Qadr* is the key doctrine of Allah's complete control over the fulfilment of events, or Destiny. This is famous for being one of the most difficult of all theological problems. It is not a problem limited to Islam – the same complicated arguments have raged throughout Christian history. How does one balance the idea of God the Omniscient with the notion that a human being has been granted freewill? If God knows in advance everything that will happen to a person, then that person's life must be entirely predestined. Furthermore, if God does not intervene to stop particular courses of action or their outcomes, then one can say that He alone is responsible for them. The problem of freewill versus predestination is linked to the problem of *theodicy*, or the problem of evil. Who is responsible for evil if God is ultimately responsible for everything? This leads to such cases as a thief pleading his innocence because he was surely predestined to steal.

Many people believe that Muslims are fatalists who believe that 'everything is written' and that God knows everything in advance – therefore it must all be predetermined. No human brain has been able to untangle this problem satisfactorily, but it is a mistake to assume that Islam is a fatalistic religion. Fatalism is an abuse of Islam; the fact that God sent revelations to humanity through the mediation of chosen prophets indicates that humans are expected to listen, make choices, and adjust their lives accordingly (Surah 6:91; 23:73).

Freewill is the fundamental ingredient of human activity, and the most difficult of God's gifts to understand or appreciate. Freewill makes sense of human morality. Without it there is no such thing as good or evil conduct, for we should simply be automatons.

The whole concept of future judgement depends on personal choice and responsibility. Even if you argue that from the outset God always knows what the ultimate fate of each individual soul will be (which He must do if He is omniscient), and that He allows each soul a lifetime as a human in order to prove it to himself/herself,[15] it does not answer the question of *why* God should choose to go through the exercise.

The most satisfactory conclusion is that God does indeed know everything and every possibility, but humans do not. Therefore, if a human chooses a particular course of action, there will be a particular outcome leading to a particular conclusion. If the human chooses a different course of action, then the outcome and conclusion will be different. For example, if you choose to swallow a whole bottle of painkilling tablets you will die this afternoon; but if you choose to swallow only two, it may cure your migraine and you may live to be a hundred. God, like a 'master-computer' knows all the possible outcomes, but He leaves the choice to you. One relevant passage in the Qur'an states: 'Truly, Allah does not change the condition of a people until they change what is in themselves.' (Surah 13:11). This certainly seems to indicate that humans have the power to change through their own freewill, and that these decisions alter their fate.

That is not a perfect answer, but no-one has ever offered a perfect solution to this problem. The real answer lies in the realm of *al-Ghayb*.[16] All devout believers can do is to ask for guidance along their path of life. They may not be able to see the road in the distance, but they pray that God will show them the steps they must take.

Belief in the Life to Come

Compared with non-believers the fact that Muslims all believe in the reality of souls and that our lives are eternal, places a different emphasis on the value of life on earth – as it does also for a true Christian. Muslims accept that the purpose of human life is to test us. *All* people will suffer at some time or another, some appallingly. Occasionally, you hear ignorant people suggest that their suffering or misfortune is in some way a punishment from God for something they have done, or even something that someone else did. Suffering should *not* be regarded as a punishment from God, or the result of lack of faith, or of not praying hard enough. One has only to think of the appalling sufferings inflicted on the Prophet Muhammad, or on the Prophet Jesus. Our suffering is certainly not caused by God but the natural result of living on a physical plane in the natural world. Moreover, Islam teachs that through physical and other sufferings Allah remits minor sins of the believers.

What is important to Muslims is how they bear the tests. They try to develop the quality of *sabr* or patience. If a Muslim gets cancer, for example, because he is human he will ask to be made better, but because he is Muslim he will also accept that if this is not to be, he should bc able to give an example of patience and cheerfulness in adversity, and not cease to love the God who is his only real support in time of trouble, and in whose presence he lives every moment of the day.

God does not take away the storm for us, but He gives us peace in the midst of the storm.

After our earthly lives have run their course, which is known only to God – Muslims believe that they do not cease to exist, but will enter a new state of existence known as *akhirah*, or the Afterlife. Once again, such a belief cannot be proved, although most religious people will argue that a fair deal of circumstantial evidence exists.

Whether or not you believe in the Afterlife, it plays an important part in your earthly life, because it provides a very real motivation for your conduct. It is the biggest deterrent of all to any Muslim who contemplates doing wrong. So what if you steal, and have your hand cut off? You can live with one hand. But what about your fate in the Life to Come? When you believe that God sees and knows everything you not only do, but also think, it alters every aspect of life. The true Muslim motivation, however, is not fear, or to earn 'pie in the sky', but genuine love for

God. Those motivated by fear, or by desire for reward, are not fully aware of the nature of God as expressed in Islam.

Belief in Judgement, Heaven and Hell

Muslims believe that after death the soul enters a period of waiting time, the length of which may be centuries in earth time, but for the 'dead' will pass without sense of time. Life does not just cease to be, even though the fate of the body is to rot away and disintegrate by one means or another. Whether the human body is buried, burnt, drowned or blown up it makes no difference to what goes on in the world of the soul, or at what time in the future the human body will be resurrected. Muslims, like Christians, believe that no-one knows the day or the hour – only that it will come at an unexpected time.

Some people feel that once a body dies the human experiences stop. All sufferings cease in a peaceful oblivion. The body is 'resting in peace'. Others suspect, from accounts of people who have had 'near-death' or actual 'death-bed' experiences, that life does not cease at all, but one enters an entirely new sphere of existence, which will be pleasant or unpleasant depending on the sort of person you were when you died.

Muslims believe in the state known as *barzakh*, the waiting period that comes between the moment of physical death and the resurrection that comes at the time of Judgement. During this period people's experiences will be different; it is believed that those who lived good lives will be able to travel enormous distances in soul-state, enjoying various pleasant and enlightening experiences; whereas those who were bad will be confined to the grave, a terrible fate, but worse may come, of course.

The Day of Judgement, or Day of Resurrection, is the time when souls are reunited with their bodies – not their earth bodies, but an entirely new creation, beyond our present understanding. The Qur'an teaches that we will be created in forms we know not of.[17] Even if people scoff at this idea or reject it, Allah says that He would restore us "*even to our fingertips*" (al-Qiyamah 75: 4). At this stage many of the bad and unrepentant will be terrified and will now realise that whereas on earth they had the freewill to believe in Heaven and Hell,or whether or not to believe in the Reality of God – that freewill is no longer available to them; they are *in* the future state, whether they like it or not, and will be obliged to face up to everything they did.[18]

For the first time they will truly realise the significance of everything they did, and the effects of their actions on others. It may be a delightful, or a horrendous, moment of enlightenment. No-one will be able to protest – each soul will have its own book recorded by the angels. This book will be opened – not to inform God – He knows everything anyway – but to justify what will come next to each soul involved.[19]

We are assured that the judgement on us will be absolutely fair and just – and moreover that no person will be able to excuse or buy another off, and that we will not be made to suffer for the sins of anyone else.[20] Every injustice will be accounted for. Those who have sinned, will have those wrongs put right by God before they can go any further. They will not 'get away' with anything they thought they had hidden. No least injustice will go unresolved.

Souls will then be sorted out, and will go to their future state of existence either Heaven (*Jannah* or Paradise) or Hell (*Jahannam*). We have also specifically been told that these matters lie beyond our capacity to understand.[21]

We'd rather think that everyone (including living creatures that we love, like our pets) goes to a 'better place' when they die. Many well-meaning graveside comforters encourage the mourners to believe that this must be so. However, on at least one occasion the Prophet pointed out to mourners, who were highly confident that their loved one would by now be receiving his rewards, that they had no right to assume this to be so – only God Himself could judge our lives, which sometimes appeared to be good, but which might have given this impression through the skill of the individual at hiding his or her real motives. Good and evil deeds done 'by accident' cannot really count as moral or immoral acts. God looks to the motives as well as the actual events.

Many believe that if we have not arrived at 'perfection' when we die, then surely God will allow further scope for progress or purification when we arrive at the stage of greater knowledge after death. Hinduism and Buddhism use the concept of reincarnation to solve the problem of those who had failed. The souls of those who had died were born in other bodies and got a chance to try again. They reasoned that a loving God would *never* send a person to Hell. However, thinking that is rather like saying that a loving teacher would never give a student an 'F' grade. The teacher is simply marking a level of attainment. If the student refuses to attend class, doesn't do the homework and performs miserably at every test, the 'love' of the teacher does not override the 'will' of the student. The teacher is not 'giving' the failed grade but rather the student has chosen a failed grade through his or her own wilful actions.

What happens to those who choose by a deliberate act of will to go *down* the 'ladder', or not to go up the 'ladder', or who may not even realise that a 'ladder' exists? If everyone ends up enjoying sweetness and light in the Afterlife, why bother with the struggle to spiritual progress now? If the devil can convince people that they do not need to struggle through their own greater jihad, he has won.

Jesus taught that there are those who love darkness and evil, who hate the light and refuse to come to it (John 3:16–21). They send themselves to Hell because they refuse to accept the love of God.

Jesus made it very clear that there was not just one form of Afterlife for all who died, but two, and that the chasm separating them could not be crossed (Luke 16:19–31). Moreover, he stressed that the testimonies of those who experience the visitation of spiritual beings, guides, death-bed visions and the like, have little impact on the realities of life after death. We believe what we believe. We have no scientific proof. We still have to approach our own deaths and the Hereafter with faith, hope and trust. Jesus remarked that we would be far better off placing our faith in what Moses and the other prophets had said rather than in these 'psychic' happenings.

So, all believers in God are happy and grateful for the concept of Heaven/Paradise. What is different between the faiths is the conclusion concerning what it takes to *get to* Heaven. Jesus made that clear too – it was to believe in the One True God, and in himself who had been *sent*. Muslims accept that Jesus was one of the many prophets or Messengers to be sent.

Hell is not God's punishment for bad behaviour, but the destination for those who find themselves separated from God's presence because they refused to accept His grace, His offer of forgiveness. Many appalling and terrible sinners do not end up in Hell at all – because they repented, were genuinely sorry, and cried out to God for forgiveness towards the end of their lives. The way to a new heart and a new life is through accepting and loving God. We are transformed even as we accept the fact that God loves us, and we begin to live within God's love.

We must recognise that each action we take in our life has the potential for eternal consequences, and the action with the *most* potential is to choose to submit to God's will, believing His purposes are being fulfilled in our lives, regardless of the difficult circumstances we sometimes encounter.

We have the responsibility to respond to God's initiative through our freewill. Some with a naive idea of predestination think that despite their actions, they will end up in Paradise because God has destined them to do so, and that others are born for Hell. But our eternal fate is *not* sealed at the time of our physical birth, only at our 'new birth' at the time of our physical death. So long as we are alive and have not hardened our hearts to the point where we can no longer acknowledge the compassionate love of God, we are capable of receiving His gift of eternal *falah* (well-being), repenting our sins, and leading a new life.

Moreover, the prophets never gave the impression that the road to Heaven would be easy. As Jesus said, the Way is narrow and those that find it are few. It involves struggle, hardship, and self-denial. (This idea is in total opposition to that presented by the Deuteronomic editor of the Old Testament. Here it claims that those with whom God was pleased would enjoy success in their earthly lives and be protected from harm and misfortune, while the wicked would be punished. That this is incorrect seems so obvious now, but the editor in question intruded his opinions throughout the books of Torah, misleading people).

So we must expect both Heaven and Hell – but we have no idea how long resurrected people will remain in these states. Some people think the final states will be for ever – but not everyone agrees. All Muslims *do* agree that it will be for as long as God will[22]; all a sinful person can do is to hope for the mercy of the Compassionate One.

What do Muslims mean by *dhikr*, or 'remembering' Allah?

Muslims strive to remain conscious of God all the time, morning and evening, day and night, through all the normal activities of life. At the same time, they do not wish to withdraw from normal life, except in certain circumstances. Muslims wish every action and thought to be permeated with the remembrance of Allah. *Dhikr* is the practice of bringing God to remembrance.

Some Muslims practise remembrance in a ritual way, perhaps by chanting phrases, or adopting certain positions, or by setting aside specific time for prayer and contemplation. For example, everyone has heard of the whirling dance of certain Muslims called 'dervishes', a dance which is supposed to bring about trance-like states. Others opt for the rhythmic chanting of phrases, sometimes accompanied by drumbeats or physical swaying, all of which induces a kind of self-hypnosis.

Most Muslims are very wary of any practice in which a person loses normal consciousness, becomes subject to powerful emotionalism, seeks to experience psychic phenomena, or tries to 'become one' with anything. There is nothing wrong with the desire to draw closer to Allah, and to love, praise and worship Him – and many of the Sufi teachers were Muslims *par excellence*, models of true spirituality, devotion, and compassionate living. The danger lies in being misled by Satan into paths of a rather selfish spiritual pleasure, a feeling of gratitude and contentment at having arrived at such a superior state of piety – and most insidious of all – the desire for closeness to God the Beloved One resulting in the chipping of the dividing line between Creator and created.

True Islam is always based on the study of that which God specifically revealed, reasoning in keeping with it, plus noble conduct and loving kindness; it is not based on emotion or all-too-fallible intuitions or 'psychic skills'.

However, there are four principles, or states of consciousness, that can enable any person to remember Allah in a deep and meaningful way, and these are true Islamic *dhikr*.

The first is to be aware that we are always in the presence of Allah. Muslims believe doubt that even if they cannot see Him, He can see them. There is no evading His presence. He is with every person, no matter where they are. (Surah 58:7). He is nearer to you than your own jugular vein (Surah 50:16–17). He sees everything you do, and hears everything you say. If we remember that God is with us, wherever we are, whatever we are doing, we are on the right path.

Secondly, we should reflect on the *barakah* or blessing of Allah, and be thankful to Him for all that He has given us. A sense of gratitude is called *hamd*, or thankfulness. The name Muhammad is derived from this root. Everything we have is thanks to the grace of God. If your heart beats 72 times each minute, it does so only with the permission and blessing of Allah. The moment He withdraws that permission, the heart stops beating and your life comes to an end.

Thirdly, we should remember that nothing in this world can happen without His permission. Everything is within His power. No harm can befall you unless Allah has wished it; no benefit can reach you unless Allah has wished it (Surah 6:17). One of the Prophet's prayers was: 'O Allah, whatever You want to give me, no-one can stop it from coming to me, and whatever You want to prevent from coming to me, nobody can give it to me.' This awareness brings serenity, courage and consolation, for your death may not come to you until Allah wills it; and when He wills it, nothing can prevent it.

Fourthly, Muslims remember that they will return to Allah when their time-span is complete, and that could be in the very next moment. We do not know when that moment will be. The hour in which you are reading this text could be your last; the time you last saw your loved ones could have been the last time; you may not see them again this side of Judgement Day. It is a sobering thought and makes us realise that every second of our lives is a gift from Allah, and not our right.

Thinking of these four things is basically how Muslims remember Allah at every moment of their lives. The purpose is not spiritual aggrandisement, or the enjoyment of an altered state of consciousness, with its attendant psychic phenomena, but to continually remember God's will, His commands and His purposes for us. The purpose of *dhikr*, or remembering God, is to help us to obey God and thus achieve inner peace.

Do we stay married in Heaven? What happens in cases of polygamy, or where people have married more than once because of death or divorce?

Christians might like to compare the answer Jesus gave when asked if a woman had been married seven times, which husband would be hers in heaven? He replied that in the resurrection they 'neither marry nor are given in marriage, but are like angels in heaven.' He then added that 'dead' people were certainly not dead, but still living. (Mathew 22:30–33).

Islam teaches that in the life to come we will be resurrected in forms unknown to us. Our mode of living will be beyond our present comprehension. When we consider the implications of the word 'marriage', we have two things in mind: a very close and binding friendship with another person and of sexual intimacy. So far as we know, in our Life to Come our bodies are not physical in the way that they are now. Such things as eating, drinking, evacuation, and sexual intimacy will not exist, certainly not in the ways that we now recognise them.

On the other hand, the Qur'an does suggest that we will be in the company of those we have loved and continue to love. It is easy to forget that many marriages are *not* blissfully happy, and the thought of being tied down throughout all eternity to a spouse one detests is horrifying. Moreover, in a society that makes so much of romantic love, the notion of physical marriage can become rather selfish. All too often one hears the phrases 'you *belong to me*' and 'I need you'. Mature and genuine love never craves for another individual or puts personal need before that of the loved one.

Western people also think it impossible to love more than one person at once; and yet surely any parent will cheerfully admit that it is quite possible to love more than one of their children at once! It would be possible to marry many times, for all sorts of reasons, and to love *all* the spouses. The fact that Islam permits polygamy in certain circumstances simply fits in with this general notion.

Notes

1. I am thinking historically of the Borgia Popes, and priests who 'sold' places in Heaven and granted forgiveness of sins at a price. Also, we might include clergy in authority who did *not* speak out in defence of the persecuted, whether blacks in South Africa or the USA (can we ever forget the shameful burning fiery crosses of the Klu Klux Klan?); those who appeased the Nazis; those who defended the practice of slavery. Perhaps today we might also include clerics who have indulged in child abuse.
2. I am thinking of such things as the Inquisition, the burning at the stake of dissenters, and witch-hunts.
3. The history of Islam is similar. Many of the individuals branded as religious terrorists by the media consist of fervent people who are sick and tired of the corrupt, money-grubbing, and exploitative leaders, who call themselves 'Muslim'.
4. Those who do not believe in God as the origin of the Universe suppose it to have existed from infinity. In other words, had no beginning. It's easy enough to claim this – it can hardly be proved (any more than the existence of God as the First Cause can) – but it defies our logic.
5. There is no proof that what started off all the movement in our universe was a Divine Being. Maybe it was the impetus of the Big Bang, the primal cosmic explosion?
6. If your parent had sneezed at the wrong moment, it might not have been you but some other sperm that fertilised your mother's egg, for example. Needless to say, by 'you' in this context, I am talking about you as a physical body – whether or not your soul existed independently of your body before you were born, and what plans God might have for you had such a thing happened, are a different matter altogether. We might call these 'contingency' plans.
7. Why call it God? As before, this cannot be proved. It may have been some force of science that had nothing whatsoever to do with a Divine Being.

8. Unfortunately, there is a descending scale of values as well as an ascending one. Bad, worse, the worst. If you argue that God is the Supreme Good you must also accept that 'He' is the Supreme Evil. If you just pick and choose which of the virtues you will apply to God, that is your personal choice. This leads to dualism, and all other sorts of speculations.
9. The goal might simply be the perfection of that form of life in its environment, which might, of course, lead to its total destruction if the environment should suddenly change. For example, the dinosaurs of prehistoric times were wiped out, and many modern species are threatened by human activity.
10. If you think God needs to be begged not to do a particular thing, then you really believe that you know better than God. If that is true, then let us all worship you and forget God, since you are obviously more worthy of that worship.
11. The Prophet's companion Umar (the second caliph) once saw the angel *Jibril* (Gabriel) in conversation with the Prophet. The only thing he remarked on as being unusually non-human was the exceeding whiteness of his clothing which for a man who had supposedly come out of the desert, was odd.
12. See Surahs 6:61, 50:17–18, 82:10–12 etc.
13. At the end of the salah prayer, while the Muslim is kneeling, he/she turns the head to right and left saying *asalaam aleikum wa rahmatullah.* This is not a greeting to the person next to you, but to your angels, who are thought to be hovering near your shoulders.
14. There are several passages where it says 'all the angels bowed down, except *Iblis*' (another name for Satan). However, this passage did not imply that *Iblis* was an angel but meant that he was present when the angels bowed down except *Iblis* the *jinn* (Surah 2:34; 7:11–18; 17:61–65; 20:116–123). Surah 15: 28–31 clarifies it – 'the angels prostrated themselves, all of them together; not so *Iblis*, he refused to be among those who prostrated themselves'. Surah 18:50 specifically states that *Iblis* was one of the

jinn; and surah 38:71–85 says he was made of fire, which was what *jinn* were said to have been created from, as opposed to angels, who were created from light.

15. This doctrine is virtually identical to the Calvinist doctrine of predetermination.
16. *al-Ghayb* refers to all matters and aspects of Allah's creation that lie beyond human understanding. Like an iceberg, only a small percentage is seen; a vast quantity is unseen by us.
17. Surah 56:60–61.
18. Surah 23:99–100.
19. Surah 17:13–14.
20. Surah 35:18.
21. Surah 32:17.
22. Surah 11:107–108

Section Two

The Religious Duties of Islam Explained

What is meant by the phrase 'the pillars of Islam'? What are these pillars?

The 'pillars' are the five tasks that Muslims have been asked to perform as compulsory religious duties – bearing witness, prayer, sharing wealth, fasting and pilgrimage. The Arabic names for these things are *Shahadah*, *Salah*, *Zakah*, *Sawm* and *Hajj*. The first, *shahadah*, has already been discussed in an earlier section.

What is special, or different, about Muslim prayer?

Muslims actually have two sorts of prayer – their five special prayers they call *salah*, and a more generalised sort of prayer they call *du'a*. *Salah* is the compulsory prayer, and is the one you will see lines of Muslims performing with various actions, including standing, bending at the waist, kneeling, and prostrating themselves with their foreheads touching the floor. Muslims are asked by God to perform this ritual prayer five times every day, at certain specified times.

Du'a prayer, on the other hand, is what all Christians would recognise as the general awareness of God's presence throughout the day, and the natural requests any human being might make to Him for help, healing or forgiveness or to thank Him for blessings and mercies received. These prayers can be said anywhere and at any time.

Salah requires certain movements and words, and has to be done in a state of purity that involves being prepared first by a ritual washing known as *wudu*, and by wearing clean clothes, if possible.

The purpose of *wudu* is not to remove dirt, but to enter a pure state, including a pure state of mind and concentration. If a Muslim has had sexual intercourse, just finished a period, given birth to a child, or been in contact with a corpse, a full bath is required before that Muslim can pray *salah*. This full bath is known as *ghusl*. At other times, the *wudu* involves washing hands, wrists, faces, nostrils, ears, head, neck, and feet up to the ankles. Women do not usually wear make-up at *salah*-time, for obvious reasons. If feet are washed carefully before the first prayer of the day, and then clean socks or tights put on, it is not necessary to remove these socks or tights at later washings – to pass a wet hand over them is enough, although some Muslims would regard this as lazy.

All Muslims start the day by praising God. If they are keeping the prayer times properly, their first prayer, and act of dedication to God, will be before sunrise. This prayer is known as *fajr* and is sometimes called the 'dawn'prayer. However, many people do not know the difference between dawn and sunrise – there is quite a long period of time between the two. Dawn, to a Muslim, means the 'first light', that which awakens the birds, and makes the cockerel crow. While the rest of the world sleeps, the *ummah* – the family of believers – will be on its knees adoring God. If this prayer is missed by oversleeping, Muslims pray as soon as they get up.

Other prayers are *zuhur* (at lunch-time, just after the sun's high point – which is not necessarily at noon); *asr,* (mid-afternoon, when the shadows are lengthening); *maghrib* (early evening, just after sunset and before it gets dark); and *isha* (during the hours of darkness). Muslims do not pray at the exact times of dawn, midday or sunset, because these moments have connotations of pagan sun-worship.

Muslims are expected to pray together in congregational Prayers in mosques, whenever that is possible. This is regarded as preferable to praying alone. To pray alongside other believers involves extra effort, self-sacrifice and organisation, and has the benefit of increasing the feeling of solidarity and brotherhood. Obviously, to do this, it is necessary to have a time-table so that people may congregate at the same time. Many Muslims (especially Muslim women, who make up over half of all Muslims) pray alone, either at these time-table times, or at convenient times within the time limits. All the prayers are valid, so long as they fall within the set periods of the day. The Prophet Muhammad made this quite clear in his lifetime by one day going out to lead the prayers at the earliest possible time, and another day at the latest possible time, and explaining that the prayers were all valid within these limits. However, the Prophet made it clear that it was *always preferable* for Muslims to pray in congregation together. It was the normal practice in the Prophet's era for Muslim women to go to the mosque and form prayer lines behind those of the men, as is still the practice in the Prophet's mosque in Madinah.[1]

Some concessions are made to Muslims. Women are not obliged to leave their families to go to the mosque, which creates problems if there are young children to take care of. People away from home can combine certain prayers; those unable to perform the movements because, for example, they are on an aircraft or in a tube-train, could pray at a later time. It is not good Islamic conduct to disturb and inconvenience others by the performance of prayer.

Do Muslims have any Clergy?

No, it is not. A priest is a person who has been specially ordained, and who lives a life set apart from that of other people; he (and these days, she) acts as an intermediary between God and humanity. A priest represents humanity, addresses God and asks for forgiveness on behalf of the people. In the old sacrificial system it was the priests who knew the requirements and rituals to make the sacrifices. In Christianity, the service of Holy Communion, or Mass, represents the sacrifice of Jesus' own body and blood, and the priest retains the function of intermediary as well as leader of the service.

This was not always the case. When the worship of the One True God was originally practised, making sacrifices to Him was not the prerogative of a priesthood. Any person could do it. People stood before God without a human intermediary.

This is the main reason why the Nonconformist groups split from the Roman Catholic Church. They too felt the importance of an individual's personal relationship with his or her Creator.

It is the same in Islam, which has no priesthood. When non-Muslims read of the various names given to the categories of Islamic scholars in various parts of the world – names such as Ayatollah, cleric, Mujtahid, Mullah and Qadi – they should realise that none of these titles refers to a priesthood. An Imam is not an ordained man, but simply any respected person who can lead the prayers. Sometimes being an Imam has become a paid job, but this is for the convenience of the local community and is not really recommended. Anyone with knowledge of the prayer of Islam may lead it, even a young boy, if he has the ability. Ladies do not lead the prayers if there is a man available, but they may certainly lead other women and children. They lead from the centre of the line, and not from a position in front of it.

In Shi'ite Islam[2], there is another concept of Imam – as the supreme leader, a descendant of the Prophet, who is considered to have special supernatural guidance. Shi'ites divide into two main – groups the Seveners and the Twelvers; the Seveners believe in the first seven Imams who were descendants of the Prophet through his daughter Fatimah, and the Twelvers accept the first Twelve. After these the Imam disappeared in mysterious circumstances, and is believed to be still alive, beyond our understanding, and guiding the faithful. Another sort of Shi'ite Imam is the eminent scholar and prayer-leader who fulfils the same role as the Sunni Imams. The highest of these are known as Ayatollahs, or 'shadows of God'. The majority of Muslims do not accept these Shi'ite beliefs and do not regard these as part of Islam as the Prophet taught it.

What is the 'religious tax'? Is it the same as the Jewish tithe, or the Christian covenant subscription?

This is the setting aside of a certain proportion of one's wealth to help others less fortunate than oneself. It is known as *zakah*, from the word meaning 'to purify'. Muslims are expected to purify their property by rising above avarice, greed and selfishness, and not clinging to too much personal gain. It is not forbidden for a Muslim to be wealthy, so long as that wealth has been honestly and honourably acquired. However, it is a strong part of Muslim culture to be generous and hospitable, and those prepared to give away that which they own are always much admired. The contribution made by the rich to the poor is particularly important in societies that have no state welfare system.

This personal 'tax' is not the same thing as being stirred to give charity through some emotional appeal. Charity in general is known as *sadaqah*, and is also highly commendable. The *zakah* is something that needs to be given regularly, and is usually levied once a year, often in Ramadan. It follows the same sort of principle as the tithe or covenant subscription, but there are certain differences. The Jewish tithe is no less than a tenth of one's income, and since this is a hard sacrifice for many people, it all too often falls into abeyance, and is therefore impractical. The Christian covenant subscription can be any amount, and does not necessarily bear any relationship to the person's income or accumulated wealth.

Once Muslims have gained a certain level of affluence (known as the *nisab)* God requires them to be unselfish and donate some of it to others. Fixed rules are laid down regarding the exact amounts that should be given up (this wealth could be in livestock, crops or mining produce, for example) and to whom this money should be paid. The recipients might be the poor and the needy, the sick and those in prison. The administrators of *zakah* may be paid out of the funds.

The rate of *zakah* is 2.5% of income, once the Muslim's personal and family needs have been met.

The object is to limit the withdrawal of money that would do more good circulated in society. If wealth is just being 'saved' by an individual, nobody is benefiting from it.

The *zakat-ul-fitr* is another payment made just at the end of Ramadan, specifically for the purpose of enabling poor Muslims to keep the feast.

References to the *zakah* can be found in surah 2:95, 210, 264, 270 and 9:60.

What is meant by fasting?

Muslims are required to practise self-discipline by making a month-long fast each year. The Muslim word for fasting is *sawm.* In the Muslim calendar, the month of fasting has the name *Ramadan*, and this is the word most westerners have become familiar with, although it really refers to the month and not the fast as such. This month does not coincide with any particular western month, as it is based on the lunar calendar and so it comes round eleven days earlier each year.

The month of Ramadan is a very special time for Muslims. For twenty-nine or thirty days, depending on the sighting of the new moon, Muslims try to set aside the trials and tribulations of everyday life in order to create a special season of holiness and peace. It is a time to concentrate on prayer and study of the Qur'an, to turn aside from cares and ambitions in order to draw close to Allah and dedicate lives, hearts and motivations to Him afresh.

Muslims make a special effort to establish peace, harmony, compassion and love. Those who have quarrelled should seek reconciliation; it is a good time to contact old friends and acquaintances who have 'wandered away'. Family ties assume fresh importance, and it is good to establish or renew contact with those who have perhaps left home or have even emigrated. When gatherings of family and friends occur, the stranger, the wayfarer, the refugee, the orphan, the bereaved, and the beloved and never-forgotten dead, should also find their share in Muslim thoughts and hospitality.

The rules for fasting are stringent. Muslims are required to abstain from just before dawn until after sunset, from all sexual activity, food and drink. Nothing should enter the body, even such things as cigarette smoke. These restrictions end at sunset, when the fast is broken with some light refreshment, such as a sweet fruit drink, and the evening prayer.

These rules all help to teach discipline, to consolidate a feeling of community amongst the Muslims, and also to show what it means to be poor and hungry, and so make compassion a bit more meaningful.

More importantly, fasting, as mentioned in the Qur'an, infuses taqwa (piety, God-consciousness and fear of God).

During Ramadan special prayers known as *tarawih* take place at the mosque after the regular night Prayer, *Isha*. These prayers include a complete recital of the Qur'an divided up over the thirty days of the fast. A particular night towards the end of Ramadan (many mosques choose the 27th) commemorates the *Laylat al-Qadr* (the 'Night of Power'), on which the Qur'an was first revealed to the Prophet.

Sometimes people following the Prophet's example withdraw altogether from normal life for a certain period, often the ten days at the end of Ramadan. This is called *i'tikaf*. During this time Muslims concentrate solely on prayer and Qur'an study, and are supported and fed either by their families or by the community. Men in *i'tikaf* usually spend this time in the mosque, and women seclude themselves at home.

What is meant by *Hajj*?

The word 'hajj' means a journey with a special religious purpose, a pilgrimage. Muslims are encouraged to make the pilgrimage to Makkah , the city in Saudi

Arabia with the cube-shaped Ka'bah, once in their lifetime. This is not compulsory for those who are ill, who cannot afford it, or who are prevented from going due to responsibilities towards others. Muslims should not even consider making the *hajj* if they owe money to anyone. That has to be paid first.

The *hajj* always takes place two months after the end of Ramadan in the twelfth *hijri* month of Dhu al-Hijja. If the pilgrimage is made at any other time it is known as *umrah* or 'lesser pilgrimage'.

If a person who could afford to make the *hajj* is close to death and finds it has become impossible for him or her to go, they can fulfil the intention by paying for another person, or by giving an equivalent amount in charity. The person who goes in their stead would have to do another *hajj,* as their own pilgrimage.

There are several main features of the *hajj*. Firstly, one must take on the state of purity known as *ihram* (from the word '*haram*' or 'set aside') For all Muslims this means entering a state of peace and harmony, and for male Muslims, it also means discarding all normal clothing and wearing nothing but two plain white sheets of cloth and sandals. This is done whether the man is a prince or a dustman – it symbolises their equality and humility before God. It may sound a simple thing to do, but most people used to wearing western clothing find it quite a strange experience! Women wear plain, simple dress, and must leave their faces uncovered even if they normally cover them. They do not necessarily have to wear white.

The chief rituals of the hajj are the seven-times circling of the Ka'bah (known as *tawaf*), seven times hurrying between the hills of Safa and Marwa (known as the *sa'i*), travelling to the Plain of Arafat and standing at Mount Arafat (known as the *wuquf*), stoning three pillars (known as *jamarat*), and sacrificing an animal and sharing its meat (the *'Id ul-adha*).

These rituals recall events in the life of the prophets Adam, Ibrahim, Ismail, and Ibrahim's wife Hajir (Biblical Adam, Abraham, Ishmael and Hagar). The Qur'an versions of the testing of Adam and Hawwah (Eve), and the testing of the obedience of Ibrahim, are different from those in the Bible.

The Ka'bah was said to have been built originally by Adam as the first place on earth set aside for the worship of the One True God. By the time of the Prophet Ibrahim it had fallen into disrepair, and Ibrahim rebuilt it with the help of his son Ismail.[3]

The circling of the Ka'bah upon arrival (and at other times during some pilgrimages) was not a rite instituted by the Prophet Muhammad, but had taken place since time immemorial. The same practice was carried out at many other shrines. The *sa'i*, the stoning of the pillars and the sacrifice of an animal, recall the story of Ibrahim. His story differs from the Biblical account because the Qur'an states that it was his son Ismail, his only son at the time, who was nearly sacrificed, and the stoning of the pillars symbolises Ibrahim and Ismail driving away Satan the tempter, who appeared in various guises to persuade them not to go ahead with the sacrifice – to which Ismail had given his full consent.[4] Ibrahim's barren wife Sarah became pregnant with Isaac as a reward for Ibrahim's faith.[5] The *sa'i* symbolises the agonising experience of Hajir and Ismail, when Ibrahim left them beside the Ka'bah while he travelled on with Sarah and Ishaq. Hajir ran backwards and forwards between the two hills, desperately looking for a passing caravan that might have provisions to spare, until God sent the angel *Jibril* (Gabriel) to show her a spring of water – the *Zamzam* well, close to the Ka'bah. The feast of sacrifice, or *'Id ul-adha*, commemorates God allowing Ibrahim to sacrifice a ram caught in a thicket instead of his son. The meat is shared out amongst the pilgrims and the poor. These days, a huge operation involving the butchering of meat and its preservation in special freezer-lorries, enables enormous amounts to be sent to areas where there is need. Nothing is wasted.

What is that big black cube-shaped building?

That is the Ka'bah. The word just means 'cube'. It is the place towards which all Muslims turn when saying their prayers. For them, in a way, it is the 'centre of the world'. Turning towards the Ka'bah is known as facing *qiblah*. Every mosque will have something in it, usually a special niche in one of the walls, which shows the direction of qiblah. In Muslim countries you will often see arrows pointing, painted on walls in hotels and other public places or erected on the top of buildings, to show travellers the way.

The Ka'bah was not built by the Prophet Muhammad when he 'started Islam'. Islam began long before his time. He was not the only prophet but the last in a very long line of them. Tradition claims that Adam built the original Ka'bah, which was the first place of worship on earth built for God. Over the centuries it was repaired many times, and all later shrines have been rebuilt on the same foundations. The most famous rebuilding was that done by the Prophet Ibrahim and his son Ismail, and the present sanctuary preserves a rock upon which Ibrahim was said to have stood whilst building a high layer.

By the time of the Prophet Muhammad it was no longer a shrine to the One True God. The people had now become polytheists, and the Ka'bah was a 'collection point' for some 360 cultic idols and objects, including an icon of the Virgin Mary and Holy Infant. When the Prophet became ruler of Makkah the first thing he did was to rid it of all the idols, and rededicate it to God.

The present Ka'bah is built of grey stones from the surrounding hills and stands on a marble base 10" high. The corners roughly indicate the four points of the compass. The north-east (front) and opposite wall (back) are 40' long and 50' high; the other two walls are 35'x50'. In one corner there is a large rock set in silver – the Black Stone. Tradition states that it originally came from Heaven and was white; this may well refer to its meteoric origin. It was perhaps 'white' or star-like as it entered earth's atmosphere, and was then discovered as a large black rock.

The walls are covered by a 'veil' – an enormous black curtain reaching to the ground – and is fastened up at Hajj time by copper rings.[6] At the end of *hajj* the Ka'bah receives a new cloth. Inside, it is a simple room with inscriptions from the Qur'an upon the walls – the only place in the world where the whole thing is qiblah, and a Muslim could pray in any direction.

Notes

1. They did not have to pray behind them because they were inferior. Allah made it very clear that all Muslims were equal, male and female, black and white, etc. The women prayed behind the men for reasons of modesty – the prayer positions would make it embarrassing for women to pray in front of men. Another reason is that Muslim women wish to grant respect to the leadership of their men. They *want* their men to be masculine, responsible, noble and good leaders, and therefore they do not begrudge them respect, so long as they are doing their best.
2. Shi'ites represent only around 10–15% of Muslims. Islam is generally regarded as Sunni, following the Prophet's *sunnah.*

3. Adam and Hawwah were disobedient, but Hawwah was not blamed more than Adam, nor was it suggested that they could pass on their sin to their descendants. Adam and Hawwah became separated; when they acknowledged their faults and came to their senses (like the Prodigal son in Jesus' story), they begged God for forgiveness. He forgave them without condition. The wuquf or 'stand before Allah' symbolises their forgiveness, and is actually the most important part of the hajj – for without this stand being performed at the correct time, the hajj is not considered valid, and counts only as an umrah.

   Obviously, the theology presupposed in these events is directly opposed to the Trinitarian doctrine, which is based on the passing on of Original Sin, and the 'need' later for God to become an incarnate god-man in order to effect an atonement.
4. In the Biblical version the little boy was kept in ignorance until the last moment.
5. The Bible account does actually state that the sacrificial son was Ibrahim's *only* son (Genesis 27:2,12,16), and since all agree that Ismail was born first, this ought really to be seen as proof that it *was* Ismail.
6. One famous 'veil' was made entirely of mole-skins, and was donated by Kaiser Wilhelm of Prussia.

Section Three

Miscellaneous Questions

Is Islam compatible with modern science?

The Muslim creed involves no tortuous mental gymnastics. Apart from three basic 'unprovable' religious concepts – belief that God exists, belief that there are orders of creation that are not part of our physical universe, and belief in life after death – Islam does not require any person to accept any other mythology or believe unbelievable things as an act of faith.

As regards science, and in particular cosmology, Islam is not pegged to any particular theory (such as the Big Bang or the Theory of Evolution) because it recognises that human knowledge is always limited, and always in a state of flux. The lessons that science teaches today may well be overturned by future scientific advances as was the case with the theory that the sun revolved round the earth, or the belief that there was a fixed sphere into which the stars were embedded, or that the universe had a 'centre' (for a long time assumed wrongly to be the earth).

The important thing to realise is that all the wonderful discoveries of science are discoveries of *what is already there.* Science does not create, but discovers and utilises. Even though we seem to know so much about 'life, the universe and everything', we essentially know very little – a minute percentage. Moreover, Muslims regard a very large proportion of our knowledge as *al-Ghayb* – 'unseen and unknowable'. However, scientific *principles* are absolutely in keeping with Islam, and Muslims are required not to pin themselves down to any particular theory, but to seek knowledge as best they may, and as much as they can, from the cradle to the grave, and from every available source.

Therefore, Muslims will quite likely accept the leading scientific theories of the day as working principles, while always keeping an open mind. Existing scientific knowledge is not a matter of faith – therefore it is no embarrassment to a Muslim when that knowledge is revised, and earlier systems are proved wrong, or inadequate.

What is the difference between Sunni and Shi'ite Islam?

Sunni Muslims are the vast majority – about 90% of all Muslims. They take their name from the *sunnah* or practice of the Prophet, and are regarded as the orthodox Muslims. Shi'ite Muslims are a sect of Islam whose historical origins go back to those who thought the Prophet's son-in-law, Ali, should have been the first *caliph* or successor to the Prophet. The name comes from *shi'at Ali* or 'party of Ali'. Shi'ites are found mainly in the places associated with Ali in present day Iran and Iraq, in Karbela and Qom, for instance.

Ali and the Abu Bakr were the very first two male converts. Ali was one of the younger sons of the prophet's uncle Abu Talib, who, father-like, had taken him into his household at the age of eight. When Abu Talib later fell on hard times, the Prophet took Ali into his own household, and he grew up with the Prophet from the age of around four. Abu Bakr was a contemporary of the Prophet, his best friend, and his companion since childhood, a man of around the same age as the Prophet and therefore of his generation, whereas Ali belonged to the younger generation. Ali married the Prophet's daughter Fatimah, and the Prophet married Abu Bakr's daughter Aishah, so they were linked in several ways.

When the Prophet died, Abu Bakr was elected Caliph in his place, but some supported the claims of Ali, maintaining that he had been appointed successor at the gathering at Ghadir Khumm, and had been given the Prophet's ring. Abu Bakr retained his position, however, and was succeeded by Umar, then Uthman; and finally Ali. Shi'ites, however, maintain that Ali should have been the first caliph, and that the others were therefore illegitimate.

After the time of Ali the Shi'ites continued to follow their own leaders, who were all descendants of the Prophet through Fatimah and Ali, and who were known as Imams. In Sunni Islam an Imam is merely a respected man who leads the prayers. However, in Shi'ite Islam the name applies to the original Shi'ite supreme leaders. The Shi'ites soon divided into two major branches, according to whether they believed in seven or twelve of these Imams. In each group, it is claimed that the last Imam mysteriously disappeared without dying, and lives on in a mystical way, guiding the faithful in their times of need, and preparing to reappear one day to establish righteous rule just before the End of the World.

Are Muslims always fighting?

Since the Second World War it has become almost fashionable in the west to be a pacifist. In earlier times the notion of fighting for a good cause, and being a warrior for God against the forces of evil, was considered a noble ideal. In Islam these principles still apply.

Muslims are *not* always fighting; the very word 'Islam' implies peace. What Islam does do is insist that it is a good and honourable thing to fight in the defence of that which matters – and to a Muslim, God matters most. Jihad, which is usually interpreted in the West to mean "holy war" or military action for the sake of Allah, actually means striving or struggle for Allah. It has a much wider meaning than the military action, mainly as the struggle against temptation to stray from Allah's way in this life. When Jihad does imply military action, it is only justified against oppressive or corrupt tyrants, or those who deliberately seek to stamp out Islam. In other words, Muslims are provoked by injustice, and regard it as cowardice to turn a blind eye.

The decision to declare Jihad is taken very seriously. As the British chose to fight in defence of their nation and on behalf of the Jews against the tyranny of Hitler, so Muslims would regard it as their moral duty to fight for what they considered right, even if it meant the sacrifice of their own lives.[1] There can be no just peace if people still live without security from harm.

The state of military Jihad can only be declared for two valid reasons – the first is defence, and the second is the undoing of injustice. When an Islamic State is attacked, it is the Muslim's duty to defend its land and people at all costs. As regards injustice, Muslims are the vice regents of God Himself, and regard it as a religious duty to rise up and end it. They have the *responsibility* to redress tyranny and evil wherever it occurs. A war entered into to restore the balance of justice is holy.[2]

The rules of Jihad require that once the enemy surrenders, all hostility is to cease. There should be no reprisals, all prisoners should be treated humanely, and if possible, returned safely to their own families. There should be no torture, rape, or injury done to prisoners. If no prisoner feels gratitude at being captured by a Muslim, then something was very wrong with the supposed Muslim's Islam! Obviously, when abuses arise, the fault lies with the individual concerned, not with the faith.

Muslims regard human life as a gift from God. Everything ultimately belongs to God, and must be returned to Him. As Jesus said: 'No man has greater love than this – that he is willing to lay down his life for his friends' (John 15:13), or, if need be, for God. The sign of a Muslim's true submission is that, if need be, his or her life is ready to be sacrificed in the service of God. A Muslim who gives up his or her life for God is known as a *shahid*.[3]

Are Muslims extremists?

In fact, very few Muslims are extremists. Whenever extremism boils over into activity that hurts the innocent, it is never condoned by the true Muslim. The Prophet Muhammad actually spoke out very firmly against extremism, especially that which manifests itself in nationalism, and divides people. He regarded it as a form of racism and hoped that God's desire for all people to accept the faith and devote their lives to His service would unite all people.

Terrorism involves the indiscriminate use of force, which in Islam is only justified as a defensive measure. Muslim terrorists are just as evil as any other terrorists, and will have to face the same judgement for their evil actions. The Prophet would *never* have condoned the bombing of a bus and the resultant deaths of innocent people, including women, children and babies. Terrorists who think they are wonderful Muslim martyrs are deceiving themselves. When Islamic 'fanatics' strike the true Muslims are those who risk their lives to defend innocent victims against the attack, to tend the wounded and console the grieving families. The notion that such attacks are justified because 'everyone' in that society does not support Islam and must therefore be in a state of war against it, is nonsense, and a complete travesty of Islam.

Sometimes Muslim extremists are called 'fundamentalists' by the western media, and this too is misleading. A real Muslim fundamentalist is someone who goes back to the original revealed text, and takes it literally. But an extremist is someone who has misinterpreted completely the spirit of the text and the life-example of the Prophet, who never resorted to the murder of innocent people.

As regards religious extremists, any amount of devotional behaviour is acceptable in private, except when it impinges upon the rights of others – for example, wife and family, or those who need help. There is always a danger that very fervent believers may go to such lengths in their personal devotions that they begin to consider themselves better than others and may even begin to neglect their duties to others. In these cases they are allowing their personal pleasure (their devotions) to become an excuse for being selfish or lazy.

The Prophet never approved of that. Of course, God would be pleased when a person prayed or studied the scriptures but not if it was done at the expense of duties towards family, spouse, or neighbours, or made them ill and resulted in them becoming a burden to others. Such conduct would create a record not of good points ('this wonderful person prayed above and beyond the call of duty'), but of bad points ('this foolish person hurt his wife/family/friend when they had need of him').

Is it true that Muslim women cannot choose their own husbands?

In some cultures many first marriages of young Muslims are arranged by their parents. However, this does not usually mean that the people involved are strangers, or have not agreed to the arrangement. To be valid in Islam marriages should never be forced. If they are, that is certainly not what the Prophet intended, and flies in the face of his teaching. Islam does not condone the marriage of strangers.

In one instance a woman complained to the Prophet that her father had married her off to his nephew without first asking her consent. The Prophet immediately annulled the marriage. Once this was done, and the woman was free again, she said to him: 'Now I am free, I willingly consent to this marriage. I only wanted it to be known that men have no say over women in their marriages.' She had deliberately done this to establish a precedent for which many women have been most grateful ever since.

Of course, it is unrealistic for youngsters to expect their parents *not* to be concerned for their welfare. Most Muslim youngsters are quite happy for their parents to arrange introductions for them. Divorce, although discouraged, is allowed to Muslims, and is usually much more easily arranged in Islamic law than English law. If an arranged marriage ends in divorce both parties may choose their own partners should they decide to remarry.[4]

As for arranged marriages of older women, many widows or divorcees might not wish to live alone, but would have some difficulty in finding a suitable partner. Such people could turn to caring relatives, or the person of authority at the mosque, to match them with another spouse. This process is a religious version of the western match-making system.

How do Muslims Treat Young Children?

Allah recommends that all children be treated with kindness and consideration, female as well as male, legitimate as well as illegitimate and orphaned. Any child, once conceived, should not be harmed deliberately; children should *never* be brutally treated, repressed or abused in any way by their parents. Muslim children should be brought up in an atmosphere of belief and respect.

Sometimes Muslims are considered cruel possibly because some Muslim families and schools accept corporal punishment as part of their discipline; if they do, it should never be carried out brutally or unjustly. It is debatable whether or not corporal punishment is a good or bad thing. The Prophet Solomon sanctioned it ('Spare the rod and spoil the child'), and many people these days have noticed how the only generation in the UK to reject corporal punishment has allowed uncouth, selfish, loutish, and thoughtless 'monsters' and bullies to develop.

Several aspects of Muslim culture might be regarded as 'cruel' by non-Muslims; for example, children may not be given free access to TV and their viewing may well be censored; they are not allowed to mix freely with members of the opposite sex once they reach puberty, and are certainly not allowed to experiment with sex, alcohol or drugs. This usually means 'no pubs, discos, boyfriends/girlfriends.'

Such a regime may seem incredibly restrictive to people who take these things for granted, but Muslims (and many non-Muslim parents) would regard their protective attitude as good sense. It is a commonly expressed Muslim opinion that in the west a sense of direction has been lost, and that some parents have no idea how to control and protect their offspring.

Do Muslims force girls into marrying too soon?

No Muslim person should ever be forced to marry against their will, according to Allah's very clear command.

It is true that in many Muslim societies girls do marry at a young age, "marriage" in that context does not involve any form of sexual activity. Only when the age of puberty is reached, can the marriage be consummated. In the west marriage is illegal under the age of sixteen, but it is common knowledge that many youngsters begin to be sexually active as young as twelve. But, to a Muslim sex outside marriage is regarded as highly dishonourable, a very serious sin, and the cause of many problems in the world.

Therefore all Muslims are encouraged to marry honourably as soon as their sexual urges become difficult to control. Muslims are well aware that to attempt to ban sex until a person is over twenty (the common age for marriage in the west) is unrealistic once the urge has become strong in a young person.

Muslims reason that the sexual urge can be quelled by separating young people at puberty, dressing womenfolk modestly, not allowing men and women to be left alone together in case temptations arise, and instead encouraging young people to concentrate their energy on wholesome activities such as study. Muslims also discourage anything likely to build up sexual urges, which the media today shamelessly exploit. They disapprove of youngsters being allowed to watch films, TV or videos that openly show sex or the use of drugs or alcohol or to listen to pop music that is deliberately designed to awaken sexual urges.

However, if their offspring show signs of human nature overcoming self-discipline, marriage is considered to be an honourable course of action, whereas teenage promiscuity is regarded as dishonourable and dangerous and, in any case, is forbidden. Hence their occasionally expressed dissatisfaction with the UK law that prevents marriage before the age of 16.

Muslims believe that it is better to let youngsters marry at puberty rather than to supress natural desires. Such supression is not realistic, a fact which results in having to kill over a million unwanted babies every year through abortions, and subject girls to so much emotional and physical suffering. Parents who allow their children to go unprotected amongst rampant youngsters are considered foolish, if not unkind and lacking in responsibility.

Muslims consider it possible for a girl to marry as soon as she becomes technically a woman (when her periods start – which could be when she is around twelve years old), although usually when a girl marries young, the sexual side of the relationship can be left aside until she is older. Most parents these days are more interested in their children's education then in rushing them into marriage.

What do Muslims think about 'female circumcision'?

This horrible practice, which is not really circumcision at all, but is better known as FGM or female genital mutilation, has nothing to do with Islam. In fact, the lessening of a woman's sexual pleasure directly contradicts the emphasis placed on women's rights in the Qur'an, and the general teaching of the Prophet. Clitoridectomy predates both Christianity and Islam, and was part of the Pharaonic culture. It probably arose in situations where a man with a large harem of women wished to curb their sexual urges to prevent them from straying. FGM was practised in various areas that later became Muslim, and is still widely practised today in parts of tribal Africa that are not Muslim at all, as well as in the Sudan, Somalia and Egypt, which are largely Muslim territories.

The phrase 'son of a circumciser of women' was a regularly used insult in Arabic. Apparently one of the Prophet's female companions, Umm Atiyyah, used to circumcise girls when requested, and the Prophet once referred to her doing this. Some Muslim scholars presumed that since he mentioned the practice, and did not forbid it outright, he therefore sanctioned it. Nothing could be further from the truth. He ordered her not to perform the 'deep cut', which is what is practised in FGM, specifically because that was detrimental to a marriage.

If a woman wishes to have some of her private parts removed for cosmetic reasons, she has the right to do this, once she is an adult, and so long as it is of her own free will. It should never be imposed on a child, and especially not in the appalling conditions that prevail in some places.

It is a terrible thing that English women married to Egyptian, Sudanese or Somali husbands need to be alerted to the possibility that if their daughters visit these countries, they risk being circumcised through the misguided motives of a relative wishing to 'preserve the girl's chastity'. It is one aspect of culture assumed wrongly to be Islamic that requires urgent attention. FGM has now been given enormous publicity, with 'shock' films being shown to people likely to consider the practice. It has now, thankfully, been made illegal in Egypt.

Can a Muslim marry more than one wife?

Yes, he can, but it should be only under certain conditions. Around 95% of Muslim men are monogamous these days, but polygamy is not forbidden, so long as the man can afford it.

The ruling of Allah was that if any injustice was feared towards any of the women concerned, Muslims were to restrict themselves to one wife only. One of the first principles of Islam is that no Muslim should ever deliberately hurt another, and if by taking a second wife the first wife was hurt, it would be totally wrong. Needless to say, most women find the thought of another wife sharing their household intolerable; and it is only barely tolerable if the second wife has a separate house or establishment of her own. Monogamy therefore is the general practice in Muslim families.

Before Islam there was no limit on a man's polygamy, or on the number of concubines or servant girls he could sleep with whenever the fancy took him, whether the girl involved wanted it or not. It was considered not dishonourable but generous for a wealthy man to support as many women as he was able to. So it is hardly just to accuse Muslims of inventing polygamy, or excessively condoning it. Christians who know their Bible may well be aware that the Prophet Abraham had several wives, including Sarah, Hagar and Keturah; his grandson Jacob's wives included Leah and Rachel, two sisters, and two concubines Bilhah and Zilpah; King David (the Prophet Dawud in the Qur'an) had thirteen wives, and his son King Solomon (the Prophet Sulayman) was the 'record-breaker' with 300 wives and 700 concubines.[5]

The Prophet Muhammad set a good example by taking only one wife (a lady considerably older than himself) and living happily with her, faithful to her alone, until she died after a marriage of twenty-five years. After her death he never forgot her or ceased to love, or regard her as his true wife. When she died he was around 50 years old, and one of his female relatives arranged for him to marry a mature lady who would help raise his two unmarried daughters. He also became engaged to Aishah, daughter of his best friend

Abu Bakr. Aishah came to love the Prophet very dearly, and was recognised as his second beloved.

In the last few years of his life the Prophet also married ten other women, some the widows of friends, some the captive daughters or widows of defeated enemies. The Prophet's attitude was always one of kindness and consideration. Not one of these ladies was forced to accept him. Most actually proposed to him, seeking his protection and security.

After the Battle of Badr, in which many Muslim men were killed, survivors were requested to take on widowed women and their children, as far as they were able; some were too generous, so the number of women they were allowed to help in this way was limited by Allah to four. Western men who think only of the possible delights of enjoying four attractive women need to recognise that in reality polygamy usually involves taking on wives past the first flush of youth, to say the least, and if a man took on a widow, she might come with half a dozen children too![6]

A Muslim man is not allowed just to 'trade in an old model for a new one', or insult his original wife by spurning her for some new flame. Such conduct would certainly have been regarded as gross injustice, and Muslim women would have complained immediately and sought redress.

However, in some circumstances, Muslim women could consider allowing another woman into their household, or allowing their husband to set up a separate household for another woman. If, for instance, the existing wife was worn out by sickness, was suffering from severe mental illness, refused to fulfil her marital obligations or, her husband wanted to marry another woman, then a second marriage would be preferable to divorce. The key quality of a wife prepared to share her husband at a time when many women were being left without support, was extreme kindness.

Can a Muslim man divorce his wife without legal proceedings?

This is not possible in any society with divorce laws. Islamic divorce is rather different from many state laws, being generally easier and less traumatic when both parties want a divorce. Basically, while they are living under the same roof, a man has to announce his intention to divorce his wife on three separate occasions with a month in between each one. If during this time, they resume marital relations, the divorce is cancelled.

Some Muslim men have abused this law by declaring ‘I divorce you’ three times on the same occasion. This is not valid.

It is true that in societies where Islam has not been properly understood, such misuses of the *shari‘ah* or Islamic law have been known to occur – and women have indeed been divorced without their knowledge. Such instances are far less likely to happen these days. It is therefore vitally important for Muslim women in these societies to arm themselves with a true knowledge of Islam, in order that they can successfully seek legal redress in cases of abuse.

Do divorced Muslim men kidnap their children and take them away?

Once again, this has nothing to do with Islam; doubtless there are cases where non-Muslim men from other countries have done exactly the same thing. The usual procedure in Islam is for a baby to remain with the mother, and for the father to provide for its upkeep. In Islamic law the father is responsible for his children, despite the fact that the mother may have custody. Custody is usually granted to the mother, but this privilege could be removed should she remarry. Muslims generally believe that the children would suffer if brought up by a man who was not their own father. In such cases, Muslim men prefer to take custody of the children themselves, and release the mother from further responsibility.

It is not regarded as beneficial for a woman to struggle as a single parent, probably in poverty. Many Muslim judges would favour the child going to its father, if the mother was seen to be incapable of providing a decent home and education. Neither parent should be denied access.

When children were of an age to choose for themselves which parent they wished to live with, the Prophet advised letting them do so.

Do Muslim men regard women as inferior?

The problem of male chauvinism is not limited to Muslim men. All over the world there are men who regard women as inferior and treat them accordingly. The Qur'an actually makes it very clear that men and women are of equal worth, deserve equal opportunities to attain spirituality, and should be given equal responsibilities (Surah 33:35). The religious and moral duties of male and female Muslims are exactly the same.

The acceptance of female equality has never been smooth, and is often resisted in societies where men enjoy power in government, at work, and in the home, through their superior strength and earning power. This is just as obvious in cultures nominally Muslim, where Islamic equality has been misunderstood, as it is in other male-dominated societies. However, Allah ordained equality, fairness and consideration for women – in education, opportunity, property ownership and in divorce law.

Justice for women includes consideration for their physical well-being. Women who are menstruating or who are pregnant are not only struggling with pain and tiredness, but also hormonal changes and therefore deserve special consideration. Men are expected to protect and maintain their womenfolk, without denying them their rights (Surah 4:34).

However, the one assertion in the Qur'an that raises a few feminist eyebrows – states that men and women have equal rights, but that 'men are a degree above them' (Surah 2:228). The word 'but' would be better translated as 'for'; it reminds a man leaving his wife and children that he has an obligation from Allah to continue to care for his children, since he is usually financially better off.

As regards maintenance for divorced women, they should be maintained by the husband during the 'waiting period', and should have their dowries paid over to them as agreed in their marriage contracts. However, after divorce the husband is only obliged to maintain his children, not his ex-wife. The responsibility for her maintenance returns to her own family (usually father or brother) or, of course, to a new husband.

Are Muslim men allowed to beat their wives?

Certainly not! Before the coming of Islam tribesmen often felt that they 'owned' their womenfolk, and usually did not grant them equal status unless they were wealthy in their own right. A man would obviously hesitate before striking another man, but deemed it acceptable to strike women and children. The Prophet abhorred men who were violent towards women, or indeed any regarded as being in a weaker position, whether woman, child, old person or slave. The practice of physically abusing such people should *never* arise in a Muslim household. Such behaviour is highly dishonourable.

Unfortunately many men, Muslim and non-Muslim alike, do treat their women roughly, even to the point of physical harm, and this is obviously not a matter that applies only to Muslims. Sadly, there are cruel and bad-tempered men within the fold of Islam, just as there are in any walk of life. Bullies usually rely on the silence of those they abuse.

Such behaviour is reprehensible and, where the laws of the land forbid it, carries a punishment.

The Prophet commanded that no person was ever to assault the 'handmaidens of Allah'.[7] He considered it wicked to hit a woman, and never once did so in his entire lifetime. 'How could you beat a woman like a camel, and then expect to have intimate relations with her later?', he demanded.

One reason why some men beat women was to force them into sexual intimacy – something it was very difficult for a slave-woman to refuse. Islam ruled that no man was ever to force a woman into sex against her will, especially a female slave. If he wished for sexual intimacy with someone 'his right hand possessed', he was allowed to do so only if he took that woman in honourable marriage – waiving her right to a dowry by granting her freedom instead. A Muslim husband and wife have agreed to satisfy each other and supply each other's needs; but even so, a woman should not be forced. If she no longer wishes to continue with the marriage, she is to be allowed an honourable divorce and not to be kept 'prisoner'.

The only possible justification for a man physically disciplining a woman comes in one verse of the Qur'an, Surah 4:36, where a verse sanctioned a man using physical discipline on his wife *as an absolute last resort,* if she was guilty of *nushuz*. This is defined as rebellion or ill-will in the sense of deliberate bad behaviour towards a husband, including mental cruelty and deliberate persistent breach of marital obligations, and was only supposed to be attempted before the ending of the marriage, if it was felt that it could be successful as a last resort. In his Farewell Sermon the Prophet said physical punishment of a wife should only be resorted to if she was guilty of blatant immoral conduct. The punishment in this case should be done symbolically and not in a way that would cause real pain.[8]

No Muslim man ever has the right to hit a woman, out of irritation, or to force himself upon her, or to keep her in fear of him. The Prophet said: "The best of you are those who are kindest to their families".

Why are so many Muslims called Abdul? Or Ben? Or Hajji? Or Al?

It only seems like this because people do not understand Arabic – even many Muslims, who weren't born Arabs. Let us take the simplest first. Ben simply means 'son of', and Al simply means 'the'. Many football fans may have noticed this during the World Cup, when commentators kept referring to the many players called Ben this-or-that, or Al this-or-that. The prefix Ben is always followed by the name of the person's father. The prefix Al is always followed by a name that either tells you where the person's family came from, or what their family occupation is. So, for example, al-Jabali is the exact equivalent of the surname Hillman; or al-Afghani means he comes from Afghanistan. Hajji applied to a man simply means that he has made the pilgrimage to Makkah, the hajj. If it is a woman, she is entitled to call herself Hajjah. Abdul is really a conglomerate of two words – *abd* and *al*, which mean 'servant/slave' and 'the'. Put together, Abdul means 'servant of the...'. The name is meaningless unless followed by another name. For a Muslim, this other name has to be one of the many names/attributes of Allah, since a Muslim will not acknowledge servitude to anyone or anything other than Allah. Therefore, it is good for a Muslim to be called Abdul Karim or Abdul Rauf, ('servant of the Beloved One' or 'servant of the Merciful One'). To be called Abdul Muhammad is forbidden, since even though a Muslim may respect Muhammad more than any other human being that ever lived, he cannot be worshiped.

Can Muslims who live in the UK join in with Christmas celebrations?

Some Muslims marry Christians, or live alongside Christian people. At Christmas, Christians celebrate the birth of Jesus, whom Muslims regard as a great prophet and Messenger of God, but who is regarded by Christians as the second Person in a Trinitarian Godhead. Because this belief is counted as *shirk* (associating partners with God) to a Muslim, they will accept neither the worship of a human being as a god, nor the need for salvation and the incarnation of God. Therefore, it is difficult and embarrassing for a Muslim to take part in any celebration of Christmas that includes the worship of the infant Jesus, or the singing of carols that hail him as an incarnate god. This can be a particular problem for a Muslim child in a state school, where a number of the social events in the Autumn term seem to be centred around Christmas.

However, for the sake of cordial relations many Muslims are content to acknowledge the birthday of the Prophet Jesus as a special day. However, Muslims, along with certain Christian theologians, do not accept that Jesus was born on December 25th. Some Christians celebrate Christmas on January 6th, for example. The actual date of Jesus' birth is unknown. December 25th was chosen because it was already an important midwinter festival, the rebirth of Sol Invictus, the Rising Sun, three days after his 'death' at the winter solstice. Hence some Christian groups, notably the Jehovah's Witnesses, refuse to celebrate Christmas on what is really a pagan occasion, with all its pagan connotations. Most of the traditional Christmas things – the tree, the evergreens, yule log, cake, pudding, gifts, decorations, and kissing under the mistletoe, are all pagan practices and have nothing to do with Christianity.

Islam urges people to maintain good relations with others. There is no harm in giving Christian friends (or relatives) gifts if they expect them. The Prophet did not prohibit his followers from doing so. Asma bint Abu Bakr once asked him specifically if she was allowed to be especially kind and to accept gifts from her non-Muslim mother, and the Prophet recommended her to do so.

A Muslim could suggest that Christians wishing to give gifts or send cards to Muslim children or friends could wrap the gift but keep it back until the next ‘Id. If this was not possible, one could simply explain to the Muslim child that the gift had no religious value, but was simply part of the British midwinter celebrations – without which, incidentally, midwinter in Britain would be pretty bleak!

Obviously no Muslim can accept the notion of God becoming incarnate, or being born as a human being; however, there is no harm in respecting the tradition of those who are commemorating the birth of a great prophet.

Why cannot Muslims eat pork?

The short answer is because God forbade it – a prohibition that predated Islam by centuries, and was accepted by Jews long before the coming of the Prophet Muhammad, in the law given to Moses (Deuteronomy 14:8 and Leviticus 11:7–8). Incidentally, Jesus – being a Jew – also never ate pork, and he ordered his followers to keep all the Jewish laws(Mt 5:19). Yet shortly after his death, the ruling was changed, thanks to a dream experienced by Jesus' disciple, Peter (Acts 10:3–7).

Pork was declared haram (unlawful) to Muslims in Surahs 2:173 and 5:3. Apart from the religious prohibition, pork seems as a meat to contain the greatest proportion of germs and parasites, most of which are contagious and some of which are fatal. The pork tapeworm (balantidium coli), the largest protozoan affecting humans, lodges in the intestine. Trichina roundworms (Trichinella Spiralis) are now very common in Europe and the USA, and are responsible for all sorts of ill-health. Pork products treated carelessly in hot weather are also some of the most common causes of food poisoning. People who do eat pork should always cook it very thoroughly.

Because of the religious prohibition, Muslims also check whether products containing animal fat or 'shortening' include pork lard. Gelatine made from the skin or bones of the pig is also avoided by Muslims.

What is halal slaughter?

Halal slaughter is the killing of an animal by swiftly cutting its throat with a very sharp knife, and dedicating that animal to God with prayer. The intention is to take the creature's life in the *kindest* possible way.[9] If any animal is slaughtered cruelly, whether or not by a Muslim, or whether there is accompanying prayer or none, the process cannot be considered halal.

The correct practice is for the waiting animal to be kept in the best possible conditions, with food, water, shade, and other comforts. Anything less would be totally unIslamic. During its transportation the animal should be properly cared for. It should not be panicked or terrified. Once slaughtered, the carcass is usually swiftly hung up so that the blood drains out as quickly as possible.

No Muslim should ever object to visits from Royal Society for the Prevention of Cruelty to Animals (RSPCA) inspectors or those from any other animal welfare organisation. Where the inspector is quite within his rights to take action if the conditions are poor, whether or not a Muslim is involved.

Slaughtering an animal by any method is traumatic for the animal; the methods usually used in the UK involve electrocution and the firing of bolts into the brain. An animal killed by electrocution would not be considered halal. Such a death is regarded as much more cruel than swiftly cutting the throat.

As regards hunting, dogs should be trained not to kill but to hold the prey, until it may be dispatched with the knife. Muslims do not eat animals that died by goring and biting, or who were clubbed to death with a blunt instrument. Those killed with bullets or spears are allowed to be eaten.

Why do Muslims think that all the normal world wide banking systems are wrong?

Muslims are forbidden usury, loosely translated as interest and widely used in banking and financial world which is known as *riba.* Basically, riba is a means of exploiting the poor. Muslims have no objections to trade, or businesses that involve shared risk, where an investor is prepared to share the losses as well as the profits.

What is seen as grossly wicked is the evil of the 'money-lender', who takes advantage of the despairing poor, by lending them money at an exorbitant rate of interest. What usually happens is that the poor person is trapped into debt and then gets deeper and deeper in. The usurers have not really helped them at all, but use the funds they have to extort more money out of others.

Muslims despise the stranglehold that banks and mortgage societies in the west have over ordinary people. In order to buy a house, a person might take out a mortgage for, say £40,000, and end up paying back over twenty-five years, around £120,000! All the payments in the early years simply cover interest. In the Islamic system one either buys the house using one's own cash, or is given an interest-free loan. Without interest the loan can be repaid quickly.

Muslims also recognise that many banks invest money in unethical business. Profits made this way are not acceptable in Islam.

Riba includes not just interest in money-lending, however. It applies to *every* form of exploitation. For example, people are not allowed to take advantage of traders by deliberately waiting until a trader in perishable goods is forced to cut his prices and sell at a loss. On the other hand, traders are not allowed to hoard their stock to take advantage of a future shortage and raise their prices accordingly. Everything about trade depends so much on the honesty of both trader and customer; if they set out to cheat each other, it damages the whole process. Muslim traders, customers, money-lenders and receivers, should all be able to trust each other with confidence. Needless to say, a Muslim is not expected to cheat a non-Muslim either!

Were the Savage Mongol Armies Muslim?

It is important to look at the facts of history carefully. The Mongols were not a bloodthirsty Muslim army, but an enemy force from central Asia who swept through the Islamic world in the 13th-14th centuries. The most famous leaders were Ghenghis Khan (d.1241), his grandson Hulagu, and Timur the Lame (Tamberlaine). Ghenghis Khan, infamous for his brutality, slaughtered unbelievable numbers of Muslims, and burned down not only precious libraries and mosques, but entire cities, including Bukhara, Samarkand and Balkh. Hulagu destroyed Baghdad, which was then the cultural centre of the world, and slaughtered three quarters of its population. Pyramids were made of human skulls, and towers out of bodies. Hulagu actually spared the Christians, but this was because he was in league with the Christian king of Armenia, whom he hoped would help him to destroy Islam entirely. He killed the Caliph of Baghdad, which meant that for the first time in history, Islam was left without an overall leader.

It should be realised that the Mongols had nothing to do with Islam, but were its bitter enemies. Later, the Mongols were defeated by the Muslim Mameluke ruler Baybars, and gradually they converted to Islam. It is highly ironic that the good name of Islam should suffer through association with an army against whom it was actually fighting!

What about Israel and the PLO?

Muslims feel that the creation of the State of Israel, and the eviction of thousands of Palestinians who had lived in the regions the new 'state' occupied, were grievous wrongs that needed reparation. They also feel that western politicians from the First World War onwards have a lot to answer for, and were largely responsible for the whole mess. The continuing hostility cannot die down because it is based on such a glaring injustice.

The 'Palestinian Problem' had its origins in the rise of the Zionist Movement at the turn of the 20th century. Many Jews, who had been persecuted throughout the world, dreamed of having the land of

'Israel' restored to them, although it had been the home of Palestinian Arabs for longer than any Jewish occupation. Incidentally, it was not the Arabs or Muslims who drove the Jews out of their land and destroyed their Temple. It was the Romans. They built a Temple to Jupiter on the site, and prohibited Jews from entering Aelia Capitolina (the Roman rebuilt Jerusalem) on pain of death. When the Roman Emperors became Christian, Jews were allowed back. Shortly after the death of the Prophet in the seventh century the rule of Jerusalem was handed over to the Muslim Caliph Umar, without bloodshed. He was welcomed by those Jews who had returned there, and accepted graciously by the Christian Patriarch Sophronius, who appreciated his nobility and tolerance. It was Caliph Umar himself with his bare hands who began the clearance of the Temple site, which had been reduced to rubble once again. Shortly afterwards, the Dome of the Rock was built on the site and the al-Aqsa Mosque was built over the site of King Solomon's palace.[10]

If we return to the history of the twentieth century, we find that people and governments were manipulated by politicians for their own ends, and much bitterness resulted. Support for Zionism increased after the holocaust of the Second World War. One popular view was that the Jews should have been compensated by being given good land in Germany, but in 1948 the British granted them the right to live in Palestine, and a deliberate campaign began to put pressure on the Palestinians to abandon their properties. Many

Muslim/Palestinian refugees who fled to Jordan had their properties seized. New Jewish settlements sprang up everywhere, and this process is still continuing.[11] The PLO under the leadership of Yasser Arafat was only one of many resistance movements to be formed.

Christians should realise that the PLO (Palestinian Liberation Organisation) is just one of several organisations dedicated to solving the Middle East Problem. It is not just a question of Muslims having a go at Jews, or Christians. Many members of the PLO are Christians – it is a Palestinian issue, not a religious one. Yasser Arafat is a Muslim, but Hanan Ashrawi is a Christian. The original leader of Hammas (a more violent group than the PLO) George Habash was a Christian.

Are Muslims trying to take over the world?

This is not a military ambition, but a desire to see the whole world submitting to the kindness, peace and justice of the will of God. Christian missionaries used to feel (and probably still do) that it was their duty to spread the word until every corner of the earth had at least the opportunity to learn about Christianity, and gain belief and salvation. Muslims feel the same.

So far as I know, Islam is the only religion that actually teaches its adherents that it is part of their religion, and therefore their religious obligation, not to try to 'do down' other religions, but to enforce the observance of other people's religious laws, so long as their adherents live peacefully in their midst. Muslims are expected to respect and preserve their churches and shrines, and enable them to prosper in their midst.[62] All people are created and loved by God and nothing differentiates them in value except their personal achievements and virtue. All people should therefore be the object of a Muslim's care and attention, which helps them to achieve the Divine Will to the fullest extent of their personal abilities, even if they do not choose to accept Islam.

Naturally, Muslims hope to make converts, for they believe that Islam is the truth, but they do not have the right to coerce – simply to present the truth as best they can, and leave the response to each individual.

Islam stresses the need to care for relative, neighbour and compatriot, but it also seeks to check nepotism, tribalism, ethnocentrism and nationalism. The aim is to bring these tendencies under God's law, so that they do not dominate.

The *Dar al-Islam* ('House of Islam') therefore *does* seek to envelop the world and transform it, to bring it into harmony with the Divine Will – but humans must freely decide whether or not to participate in this. There should be no coercion, compulsion, trickery or brain-washing.

'Virtue and wisdom are manifestly different from vice and misguidance. Whoever rejects evil and believes in God has grasped the most trustworthy handhold.' (Surah 2:256).

Muslims are indeed called upon to bear witness and preach the word of God whenever they find the opportunity. 'Call people forth to the path of the Lord, by wisdom and sound argument. Argue the cause with them, but with pleasant arguments.' (Surah 16:125). The example of the Muslim's own lives, their personal embodiment of the truths and values they profess should constitute their strongest argument. If those who hear the message are still not convinced by these peaceful methods, Allah specifically commanded His Muslims to *leave them alone.* (Surah 3:176–7; 47:32).

This does not mean that Muslims should ever give up trying when they get the opportunity, and they should certainly never give up hope that Allah may guide those non-Muslims to the truth. If the non-Muslim is still not convinced, the Muslim should strive to better himself or herself in conduct and way of reasoning, and leave the rest to God.

Much as Muslims may hope to win every single person over, they know this will not be the case. So long as those who do not accept Islam do so in peace, Muslims are ordered to respect their points of view, and never to harass or try to coerce. If non-Muslims put deliberate obstacles in the way of the free and responsible interchange of ideas, then Islam does allow these obstacle to be removed, by force if necessary. If the enemy picks up the sword, then the Muslim may do the same. But this armed resistance of Muslims should never be resistance to the religious propositions of others – these should only be countered by better propositions. Muslims may only draw the sword against those who have themselves drawn the sword instead of accepting the principle that the best argument should win. Muslims should not regard non-Muslim territory as 'Dar al-Harb' (the House of War) but as Dar al-Dawah' (the House of Possible Converts).

Any violence committed by Muslims is only justified if it opposes violent obstruction, and should never be used in mere nationalistic causes, for the sake of aggrandisement, to punish a non-Muslim for being simply that, or to coerce a non-Muslim into conversion. You can browbeat people, you could force a person to live with and sleep in the same bed as another, but you cannot force them to fall in love with each other. Similarly, people can be forced into uttering false statements, but cannot be forced to believe in Islam. Terrorist activities, including attacks on innocent people, hijackings, kidnappings, bombings and so forth, may well arise out of keenly felt frustration, but it is no part of Islam to endanger and hurt innocent individuals to gain publicity for a cause (no matter how righteous), or to vent spleen on non-Muslims.

As regards the unification of Muslims, some have favoured the idea of *Pan-Arabism*, which seeks the unification of all Arab states into one United Arab Republic, on similar lines to the United States of America. This idea has never had much success, and really falls at the first hurdle, since its promoters seem to have forgotten that millions more Muslims are non-Arab than Arab. For example, Pakistanis, Bangladeshis, Iranians, Malaysians, and Indonesians are not Arabs. Statistics reveal some unexpected facts too – for example, everyone knows that in Pakistan the population is around 95% Muslim, whereas in India it is only around 11%. Yet such are the population sizes of each country that millions more Muslims live in India than live in Pakistan! Many Arab states are just about 100% Muslim, but because these territories are sparsely populated in comparison to other countries, the actual *numbers* of Muslims in them are comparatively small. There are millions more Muslims in Indonesia and China. Soon, just as there are many more Jews in the USA than in the 'state of Israel', there will be many more Muslims in the USA than in the Arab countries. In any case, the concept of Pan-Arabism is racist and elitist if a person's 'arabness' is to be defined by birth, or ability to speak Arabic.

A better idea is *Pan-Islam* the unification of all Muslim states under one supreme leader, a new caliph. The last caliph of all Islam was the Turk Abdul Hamid, who was deposed by Mustafa Kemal (Ataturk). Unfortunately, one of the main failings of those whose Islam is only skin-deep is divisiveness and nationalistic fervour – both of which are contrary to the spirit of Islam, so a political Islamic Union is highly unlikely. A further problem is that so-called Islamic states may actually have drifted a long way from Islam – a point most of the extremists try to emphasise, and governments concerned may unfortunately be just as corrupt as those condemned in the non-Muslim world. In any case, the notion pays no attention to the many

Muslims who do not live in Islamic states, but who would still like to have a religious leader of international repute.

Many Muslims favour some kind of return to the Madinah Ideal, which could include all Muslim individuals, irrespective of their nationality and homeland. That is certainly what I, as an English-woman, would prefer, for it would give me a chance to belong.

Notes

1. Many westerners might wonder why, in that case, Muslims do not oppose tyrants such as *Saddam Hussein* of Iraq *or Colonel Qaddafi* of Libya, while continuing to fight 'the Jews' or the Saudi royal family. The answer is that Westerners see things from a totally different point of view, and one that has been influenced by the media. Those the west thinks of as terrorists are often accepted by their own people as champions of the 'underdogs' against the might of some other oppressive power (especially the USA). The most important war in these cases is the propaganda war – and wherein lies 'the truth'.
2. As regards Iran, the Muslim sees the USA as an aggressor in harbouring the Shah, who had committed numerous crimes against his people, including the misappropriation of billions of pounds of public wealth. Muslims admire the USA for giving refuge to victims of injustice, but condemns it for harbouring the perpetrators. As regards Zionism, the Muslim view is that the Zionists are the aggressors and the Palestinians the victims of armed robbery. The Muslims feel obliged to resist that robbery.
3. Remember *shahadah* means 'to bear witness'. To be a martyr (*shahid*) is to be the ultimate witness one's belief in God.
4. I gather divorce is by no means easy in many Islamic societies, especially those where cousins are married, since divorce in these circumstances can cause considerable family trauma. Also, in some societies, divorcees (and widows) have a tough

time finding another husband. Neither of these things is the correct Islamic teaching, All but one of the Prophet's wives were divorcees or widows.

5. Polygamy is still practised by many Christians in Africa, and also by Mormons in the USA, although it is banned officially. Many women are very much in favour of it, although no women like the system to be abused. It was a very useful practice that took care of defenceless women who had no state benefits, especially at times when many men died in battle.
6. In the case of the Prophet's marriages, Hafsah came with one son, and Umm Salamah with four children. He had an *enormous* number of dependants in his household.
7. Recorded by Abu Dawud, an-Nisa'i, Ibn Majah, Ibn Hanbal.
8. The commentator Tabari suggested it should be done with a miswak (the tooth-cleaning stick), whilst Razi recommended that a handkerchief should be used.
9. 'Allah has ordained kindness in everything. If killing is to be done, do it in the best manner; and when you slaughter, do it in the best manner by first sharpening the knife and then putting the animal at ease.' (Hadith Muslim).
10. His stables can be visited even today, beneath the Temple site.
11. The Zionist expansions always involved great speed and efficiency. Populations have been scared away to be replaced by occupiers using prefabricated buildings or building materials and ready-grown trees and plants – which are then guarded as a *fait accompli*, leaving the displaced occupants to do little more than rage.
12. Where we find cases of Muslims attacking other churches, holy places and shrines, this is totally contrary to Islam (except in cases where those holy places have taken up physical resistance against Islam and are attacking it). It is the responsibility of educated Muslims to make this very clear to those who think otherwise. Needless to say, where we have cases of one *kind* of Muslim attacking another, this is terribly wrong. We have the sad cases today of Shi'ite and Sunni Muslims in Pakistan attacking each other; in several parts of the Islamic world Muslims have been slaughtered whilst at prayer by other Muslims! May God have mercy on them, and enlighten them to the Straight Path!

SECTION FOUR

Christianity and Islam

What changes of belief would Christians have to make if they accepted Islam?

a. The starting point for any person wishing to become a Muslim is a declaration known as the *shahadah*. It is a very simple creed in two parts:

> 'I bear witness that there is no God but the Almighty (Allah); and I bear witness that Muhammad is the Servent and Prophet of Allah.'

What this means is that the person genuinely believes that there is only One God, Who is 'the Almighty'. Secondly, the person has genuinely accepted that the messages revealed to Muhammad are not his own inventions or 'fakes', but the genuine messages of the Genuine One God.

Sometimes converts came into Islam in two separate stages; for example, the Prophet's uncle Abu Sufyan was able to accept the first part of the shahadah eventually (he had been a staunch pagan all his life, worshipping his ancestral gods that were kept in the Ka'bah), but it took him longer to accept the second part. [8]

It does *not* mean that Jews or Christians have to immediately cast aside all their own scriptures, but they *do* have to measure their content and teaching against the Qur'an. They will discover, of course, that virtually all the recorded sayings of the prophets are not only completely in keeping with each other, and with the teachings of Jesus, but also with the teachings of the Qur'an, since they come from the same Source, God the Almighty. However, they will also discover some things that are not in keeping,[9] and here they will have to use their reason, intellect and sense of morality if they are to see that it is the Qur'an which has the truth. Muslims maintain what Biblical scholars have argued for centuries, but which has yet to reach the mass of believers who are not exegetes, that in the other scriptures certain verses, or emphases in them, have been created (even invented or faked) by the motivation of the various human editors.

b. Many quotations from the Qur'an could sum up the Muslim faith, but the one quoted here is perhaps the most pertinent:

> *It is not righteousness to turn your faces towards east or west; but this is righteousness – to believe in God, and the Day of Judgement, and the angels, and the Book (meaning all God's genuine revelations to all of His prophets), and the Messengers; to give from your wealth out of love for God to your family, to those without family, to those in need, to the wayfarer (including the refugee), and to those who ask, and for the setting free of slaves; to be steadfast in prayer and to practise regular giving; to fulfil all the promises which you have made; to be firm and patient in pain and suffering or any other adversity, and through all periods of panic. Such are the people of truth, the God-fearing.*
>
> (Surah 2:177)[10]

This quotation speaks for itself; the various clauses in it will be examined in more detail in Section One of this book.

c. All Muslims would happily accept Jesus's reply to a Jewish religious teacher who asked him which of all the teachings of God was the most important? Jesus answered:

> *This is the first commandment. "Hear, O Israel! The Lord our God, the Lord is One. And you shall love the Lord your God with all your heart, and with all your soul, and with all your mind, and with all your strength". And the second is this: 'You shall love your neighbour as yourself.' There is no other commandment greater than these.' Then the scribe said to him: 'You are right, Rabbi.*

> *You have truly said that He is One, and there is no other but He; and to love Him with all the heart, and with all the understanding, and with all the strength, and to love one's neighbour as oneself, is much more than all whole burnt offerings and sacrifices.' And when Jesus heard that he answered wisely, he said to him: 'Truly, you are not far from the Kingdom of God.'*
> (Mk 12:28–34)

Incidentally, Jesus was not the first to use these words as teaching. He was quoting what was called the Shema, the verses of Deuteronomy 6:4. These were the very words Jews were commanded to write on parchment and place in little boxes called phylacteries, which were strapped to their arms and foreheads as they prayed, and also placed in little containers called mezuzim, which they fixed on the thresholds to their houses so that they could touch them every time they came in or went out.

Rabbi Hillel, the most famous Rabbi of the generation before Jesus, also gave this teaching. The story is that once an irritating student went the rounds of great teachers asking if they could summarise the whole of the Law for him in the time he could balance on one leg. Rabbi Shammai impatiently hit him with his builder's cubit, and sent him on his way; Rabbi Hillel told him to take up his stance, whereupon he declared that this verse was the whole of the Law; the rest was merely commentary on it.

d. Finally, I would like to refer to one of the hadith – a teaching of the Prophet Muhammad (peace be upon him) – in a story reported about him.

Once a delegation calling themselves believers came to him in Madinah. The Prophet said: 'Everything has a substance, so what do you define as the substance of your belief?' They said to him: 'We have fifteen characteristics. Five we have been told to believe in, and five you have ordered us to do, and five are our traditions. We will maintain these unless you instruct us to the contrary.'

They told him that they believed in God, His angels, His revealed Books, His Messengers, and in resurrection after death. Those were the five beliefs taught by the Prophet's representatives. Those to whom the Prophet had given instructions were to bear witness that there is no deity save Allah; that there should be prayers five times per day; payment of the *zakah* (a proportion of one's wealth set aside to help others); fasting in the month of Ramadan, and, if possible, a pilgrimage to Makkah once in a lifetime. The five among their own traditions were thankfulness, fortitude, patience, steadfastness and compassion; to be grateful in times of plenty, to remain faithful in times of adversity, to accept God's will whatever it may be, not to desert the cause on the field of battle, and not to show pleasure when calamity befell an enemy.

The Prophet commended them on these and added five more to make their total twenty. He said to them: 'If you are truly as you say, then do not amass what you cannot eat, or build what you do not reside in, nor complete what you will soon abandon. Fear God, to Whom you shall return, and work for what you will soon be facing.'

If a person could strive to keep these twenty, he or she would be truly Muslim.

There is only One True God. Jehovah (Yahweh), Our Father in Heaven, and Allah are one and the same God

The three religions of Judaism, Christianity and Islam do indeed all worship the same God, even though some followers of each faith might not have realised it, or might have been confused by the fact that they use different names for God. Every adult in the UK who grew up at school with lessons in RE (formerly known as 'scripture') is familiar with some Old Testament narratives and the fact that God is known as Jehovah in the Old Testament. The name Allah is, however, an unfamiliar one. Jehovah, of course, is just as 'foreign' to English folk, but Allah seems much more 'foreign' because this name is unfamiliar in Christian teaching. This unfamiliarity gives the false impression that Allah is a different god, a rival god – a notion strengthened of course, by past events, such as the Crusades, or the conflicts in Spain between Christian knights and the Moorish conquerors.

Christians usually accept that the Old Testament is part of their own holy literature, despite the fact that it originated long before the arrival of Jesus, and is solidly against all the manifestations of ancient worship which was generally based on a trinitarian theology with a divine Father, Mother, and dying-and-rising saviour-Son (the system usually called Baalism in the Old Testament). Christians accept that the heritage of the prophets is *their* heritage; they assume that the God who spoke to Moses is *their* God, the God, who was caring for His created people long before the incarnation of God the Son.

However, only certain groups of Christians refer to God as *Jehovah.* Most call Him simply 'the Lord', and it is all too easy when moving into New Testament times, to confuse 'the Lord' who was and is God the Almighty, with 'the Lord' who was Jesus, His Son (as Christians believe). Few Christians use the Hebrew name familiar to Biblical scholars – *Yahweh*, the name God revealed to Moses when he asked Him directly to tell him His name. Yahweh is derived from God's statement: 'Ehyeh asher ehyeh', a phrase with several choices of meaning ranging from 'I am that I am' to 'I will be as I will be' or 'I cause to be what I cause to be', or any combination of these. [1] It is not really a name, but a statement of Existence, Causality and Permanence.

As a name for God, Yahweh is as unfamiliar as Allah to these Christians. The point that needs to be understood by all is that God the Father, Jehovah, Yahweh and Allah are one and the same God. *There is only one True God no matter what people call Him. The Supreme*

One, the Almighty, can by definition only be One Alone. There cannot be two supremes. Allah is simply the Arabic word for 'the Almighty'. It is the word for God normally used by Arabic-speaking Christians as well as Muslims in the Middle East.

People who can see the connection between Judaism and Christianity may perhaps think that Islam is a 'different' religion because it has various different practices and emphases. That, of course, is true. Christians do not think of themselves as Jews, or vice versa, and both Christians and Jews do not think of themselves as Muslims. Needless to say, Muslims do not regard themselves as Christians or Jews. Their allegiances to the practices, dogmas and rituals they believe to be correct set them apart as three different *sets of believers*. Yet they are all '*Ahl al-Kitab*' – 'People of the Book', that is, receivers and followers of Revelation from the One True God. It is the same God that inspired all the prophets at different periods throughout history.

The word 'Islam' simply means self-surrender to the One True God, or submission to the will of God.

Insofar as devout Jews and Christians believe that they are truly submitted to the One True God, then they are Muslim. The Qur'an and the teachings of the Prophet Muhammad (May Allah's peace and blessings be upon him and all the Prophets) make it very clear that the great Messengers, such as Abraham, Moses, Noah, David, Solomon, John the Baptist and Jesus were all considered by Muslims to be *Muslim.*

All three faiths originated in the same 'patch of sand', the same small section of the world, and all are entirely based on the notion that this One True God really does exist, but that it is impossible for human beings to know anything about Him unless He chooses to reveal it to them.

The history of all three faiths originates in the revelation to Abraham, the Nomad of Mesopotamia, and his descendants, including Joseph, David, Jesus and Muhammad. Therefore, they certainly ought to think of themselves as belonging to one 'family'.

The respect Islam grants to Judaism and Christianity, their founders and scriptures, is not just courtesy but an acknowledgement of their religious truth. Islam does not see them as 'other religions' it should tolerate, but as part of itself – as truly revealed religion from God. In this Islam is unique – for no other religion in the world has made belief in the truth of 'other religions' a necessary condition of its own faith and witness.[2]

Moreover, non-Muslims living in an Islamic State are not required to accept Islam; in fact, their own beliefs and the right to believe them are actually *protected* by Islam. For example, after the advent of Islam a Jew could model his life on the Torah and do so supported by the public laws of the State; a non-Jewish State put its executive power at the service of rabbinic law. The State assumed responsibility for the maintenance of Jewishness and declared itself ready to use its power to *defend* the Jewishness of Jews against their enemies. After centuries of oppression the Islamic State was regarded as a liberator and protector. Jewish law, religion and institutions became a sacrosanct trust whose protection and perpetuation became a Muslim responsibility imposed by Islam itself. Only questions of war and peace lay outside the jurisdiction of non-Muslims. All this was possible because of the Islamic principle that recognised the Torah as true revelation.[3]

The same principle applied to Christianity. The Christians of Najran, for example, came to the Prophet and were invited to accept Islam. Some converted, but the majority did not. The Prophet nevertheless granted them the same autonomous status, loaded them with gifts, and sent them home protected by a Muslim bodyguard. For the greater part of the first century of the Islamic State a large number of its citizens were Christians, who enjoyed respect, liberty and a new dignity – because of the Islamic principle that recognised Jesus as a true prophet of God.

If Jews, Christians and Muslims really do all worship the same God, why cannot they just get together and become one faith?

If only it were that simple! You do not need to have interfaith committees and meetings to come to grips with the problems that arise when *this* quite reasonable question is raised. The task of bringing together all the various branches of Christianity is hard enough, and has never been achieved, not even in the primal history of the Church, when fierce differences broke out between the converted Jewish Christians led by Jesus' brother St. James, and St. Paul's mission to the Gentiles. When religious faith is involved, especially when that faith is based on different interpretations of revelation from God, feelings run very high, and people cling to their cherished beliefs and principles.

In their aims, Muslims, Jews and Christians all desire to see the will of God done on earth as it is in Heaven; to care for God's earth; and to enjoy the nearer presence of God in life after death. Islam did not appear out of nowhere, but reaffirmed the same truths as were presented by all the previous prophets of the Jews and the Christians.

Muslim and Jewish theology is virtually identical. Where Muslims and Jews are in conflict is over the concept of a 'chosen race' and the notion that a particular piece of the Middle East was granted to Jews as a 'Promised Land'. Muslims believe all human beings to be the loved creations of God and that no race is chosen above any other. All races are equal in Islam, the individual merits of people being judged by their good lives as individuals, and not by the colour of their skin, or their parentage. Muslims do not trust the Old Testament as an uncorrupted revelation from God but believe it has been very much corrupted and 'watered down' by various editors with their own axes to grind.[4] For example, Muslims do not accept that all the bloodthirsty massacres carried out under the orders of

Joshua, in his gradual conquest of the already-occupied 'Promised Land', were really the will of God. Muslims are more in sympathy with the later Judaic and Christian notion of a 'true Israel' based not on racial origin, but on the decision to serve God.

Where Muslims and Christians are in conflict is over their interpretations of the person and role of the historical Jesus. It is this difference which divides the two faiths and apparently makes it impossible to form a convenient accommodation between them. No one can declare 'I am a Christian Muslim' or 'I am a Muslim Christian'. If a Christian believes in Trinitarian theology, to state that Jesus was *not* God is blasphemy; it undermines the entire edifice (and point) of salvation theology, and renders the necessity of Jesus' incarnation and crucifixion meaningless. Certainly, if Christians abandoned the notion of Christ's divinity they would lose entirely the belief in the necessity of Jesus as a 'God-man', as a vehicle for salvation, or that belief in Jesus could bring a person forgiveness of sins and eternal life. As St. Paul bluntly put it in 1 Corinthians 15:12–19:

'If there is no resurrection of the dead, then Christ has not been raised; if Christ has not been raised, then our preaching is in vain and your faith is in vain. We are even found to be misrepresenting God, because we testified that He raised Christ, whom He did not raise if it is true that the dead are not raised...If Christ has not been raised, your faith is futile and you are still in your sins. Then those who have fallen asleep in Christ have perished. If for this life only we have hope in Christ, we are of men most to be pitied.'

The errors of logic made by St. Paul, as far as Muslims are concerned, is that he equates God's raising of Jesus to be proof of his divinity, and suggests that our faith in God and the afterlife is futile if the claim that Jesus rose again from the dead were not true. Why should *our* faith in God be futile, whether or not Jesus was raised from the dead?

For a Muslim (or a Jew) to state that Jesus *is* God is blasphemy; Islam, through the Qur'an, teaches absolute monotheism. God is One, the Absolute, the All-in-All, the Supreme. There is none like unto Him, and He should should never be thought of in human terms. He has no 'partners' or 'sharers' or 'offspring', and does not mingle in any way with created matter. Even the word *He* is misleading; rather than 'God' or 'He' Muslims always prefer to say 'Allah' – a word with no gender connections. One can have Father/Mother, or god/goddess – one cannot have Allah/Allahess or Allahs. Allah is One.

Islam gives the maximum that can be given to Judaism and Christianity. It acknowledges their founders, prophets, scriptures and teachings. It declares its God and the God of Jews and Christians to be One and the Same. It commands Muslims to be the assistants, friends and supporters of Jews and Christians, under God, protecting both them and their places of worship. It regards the differences between them as surmountable through greater knowledge, good-will and wisdom, treating these differences as 'domestic disputes' within one and the same religious 'family'.

How then do Muslims account for the differences between Jew, Christian and Muslim?

The messages of all the prophets were simple and fundamental. Firstly, they decreed that we should acknowledge that God alone is God, and all worship, service and obedience are due to Him alone. Secondly, we are required to live moral lives, doing good and avoiding evil.

Each revelation came with a code of behaviour applicable to the people for whom it was revealed, relevant to their historical situation and condition. There is therefore legitimate ground for religious variety in history. The messages are one and the same *in essence*, but the law is revealed in a way relevant to particular conditions and states of development on the human scale.

However, religion is also affected by human nature. Many simply do not *want* to do the will of God; they may have vested interests that are opposed to it. The rich may not want to help the poor. The undisciplined may not want to live disciplined lives and may rebel against the rules of law and society. Justice may not appeal to those in power who want their own way. People do not want to worship God and live unselfishly, but face the constant temptation to self-adoration and self-indulgence.

Finally, when the contents of the revelations are not meticulously remembered, taught and recorded, it is all too easy for dilution, distortion, shift of emphasis and change to creep in, not to mention mistakes, change of interpretation and downright deliberate deceit!

What about all the Christian Unitarians who do not believe in a Holy Trinity?

Most Christian people grow up in a particular church or denomination, and usually do not switch from one to another as they get older. It *can* happen, of course. As a teenager, I myself went from Church of England to Salvation Army to Quaker to Buddhist to High Anglican in my search for the Truth. People who move around the denominations do not do it out of cussedness, but because they feel unhappy with either the style of the worship offered in a particular church, the theology taught there, or the aspects emphasised. Some people like silent prayer and meditation; some like tambourines, brass bands and happy communal singing; some like forty minutes of rousing sermons; some like academic brevity and beautiful choral music, and so on. All those churches in the UK that are not Roman Catholic came about by people having strong convictions and strong preferences. Others, of course, accept the staunch discipline and devotions of Roman Catholicism – and it is easy for those belonging to a non-Roman denomination to pass their entire lives without ever visiting a Roman church, and vice versa. Many Protestants do not realise that the total UK membership of all the many denominations, is around 2 million compared with around 4 million of the Roman Church. Yet the Church of England is the Church of the Queen and the Archbishop of Canterbury, and is the one on show at public national events, such as coronations. The reason for this is a matter of recent history – just the last 400 years or so.

The Unitarians are Christians who do not believe in a Holy Trinity. They believe, as do Muslims and Jews, that the Holy Spirit is not a separate entity, but the actual spirit of God Himself when He acts in the sphere of His creation. They also believe that Jesus, although a person of the utmost importance, was a human, a prophet, and not an incarnate part of a Triune God. He was not a Son of God, but one of God's 'children', just like the rest of us.

If Muslims are surprised by the hostility and aggression encountered from certain sections of Christianity, they should be consoled to discover that the Unitarian Christians also endured terrible persecution. They suffered far more for their beliefs than today's Muslims do in the UK, for despite all the complaints, the UK remains one of the most tolerant places on earth towards people of different beliefs.

Only four hundred years ago, if anyone declared 'I believe God is One', he or she faced impoverishment, torture and death.[5]

The Unitarians 'no longer had access to the original teachings of Jesus, nor to his way of life, both of which had long been lost to posterity and were in any case superseded by the advent of Islam; but they looked at what had become of the Trinitarian Church and its doctrines, and concluded that something was seriously amiss and, after using their intellect to critically appraise the main doctrines and practices of the Trinitarians – neither of which derived from Jesus – they arrived at an intellectual recognition of the Divine Unity, especially once they had the good fortune and the courage to realise and appreciate that much of the dogma and religious practices which had been evolved by the European Trinitarian Christians during the course of many centuries, not only had not come from Jesus in the first place, but also simply did not make sense anyway.'[6]

Why is the Qur'an regarded as such a holy text?

The Qur'an is *not* the collected teachings of the Prophet Muhammad. Historical evidence suggests he could neither read nor write. The Qur'an refers to him as *'unlettered'*, but we must realise that he was a successful merchant and not a simpleton. He was certainly a very devout and highly respected man long before his call to be a prophet. His own teachings, parables and other works are kept quite separate from the Qur'an, and are known as the *hadith*. These cover many thousands of pages; some are regarded as totally reliable, while others are doubtful and may have originated in pious stories or inaccurate memory.

The Qur'an is something very different – a series of revelations from God imparted to Muhammad over a period of twenty-three years.

These revelations came to Muhammad either by a voice which only he could hear, or through the intermediation of the angel Jibril (Gabriel). When he heard the revelations Muhammad carefully memorised them and had them recorded on whatever materials came to hand by people who *could* write.[7] Later they were collected up and put into book form, the final order being something the angel revealed to Muhammad shortly before his death. This was not the order in which they were historically revealed. This book was then given into the safe keeping of his wife Hafsah, and exists to this day.

Muslims who knew the entire Revelation by heart were (and are) called *hafiz* (pl. *huffaz*). Very many of these devout scholars exist today, as they did in Muhammad's time – able to check the statement that the Qur'an has existed unchanged and unedited since Muhammad first recited it for his Companions to learn. It is a common occurrence for an Imam to err slightly whilst reciting the Qur'an during the congregational prayer and for several voices to correct him from the rows behind. This does not make the Imam angry or ashamed – anyone can make a slip. On the contrary, he is grateful for the correction. The Prophet himself was once corrected by his companion Ubayy ibn Ka'b.

The Holy Qur'an differs from any other religious text in that it was not written or edited by any human author; no word has been added to it or subtracted from it. It contains nothing but the messages as the Prophet received them. Therefore, if any part of it differs from something presented in the Jewish or Christian scriptures, a Muslim will always prefer the text of the Qur'an, as coming straight from God Himself.

Is it true that Muslims believe that Jesus and the Jewish prophets were Muslim too?

In a word, yes. To a Muslim, Jesus, Abraham and Moses were *all* Muslims – in the sense that the word 'Muslim' means someone who completely submits his or her life to the will of God. If you have read the preceding definitions of Islam, surely no-one could possibly argue that Jesus, Abraham or Moses were not outstanding examples of people who had submitted themselves entirely to God in exactly the same terms as those expressed there. Muslims believe that they were men of such piety and devotion that they were called to become Messengers of the Divine Will for the benefit of humanity.

Is it true that Muslims believe that the Prophet Muhammad was greater than Jesus?

This is not what is taught in the Qur'an, which states quite clearly that Muslims must believe in *all* the prophets, and *make no distinction between them.*

> *We believe in God, and in the Revelation given to us, and to Ibrahim, Ismail, Isaac, Jacob and the tribes. We believe in all that was given to Moses, Jesus, and all the other Messengers from the Lord. We make no distinction between them. To God Alone we surrender.*
>
> (Surah 3:84)

This means that since all the prophets were chosen Messengers of Allah, it is not for us to try to decide, centuries later, which of them were the best, or if any were greater than the others. Only God can possibly know that.

It means that Christians are not correct in thinking that Jesus was the Supreme Messenger, with a special sacrificial role of salvation; he was not a Son of God, but just one more Messenger in a very long line of Messengers. It also means that Muslims should not claim Muhammad to be greater than Jesus. Jesus had so many unique characteristics – he was born of a virgin, by God's will; he healed many and could intervene with the laws of nature, and even raise the dead, by God's will. Although many miracles were attributed to Muhammad, he always modestly claimed that the one great miracle of his life was the revelation of the Qur'an.

Christians should bear in mind that Muslims born into the faith are not nearly as familiar with the life and work of Jesus as they are of Muhammad; to them Muhammad is *their* special prophet, and they think of him with enormous veneration. Some venerate him too much, and have to be reminded that this can reach a dangerous level and lead to the same error that Christians made, in the eyes of Muslims that of turning their prophet into a superhuman, and then a 'divine' person.

No Muslim ever claims that the Prophet Muhammad was someone to be worshipped, a 'divine' figure. So, in this sense, a Christian who assumed that Jesus really *was* the Son of God would naturally assume that 'their' Jesus was superior to the Prophet Muhammad. Such a Christian would be irritated and offended by a Muslim who believed Muhammad to be 'superior' to Jesus, and would regard that as ignorance and blasphemy.

Muslims who do think Muhammad was 'superior' to Jesus can only justify this by arguing that his message came much later in history, and was intended to 'put the seal' on all previous revelations from God, including that of Jesus. Moreover, the message revealed to Muhammad was intended to correct the errors in the form of Trinitarian doctrine that had corrupted the original teachings of Jesus.

As regards Muhammad the person, or Jesus the person, to engage in some sort of competition respecting their goodness or greatness is not considered by Muslims to be a proper exercise. Muhammad was not divine, and any attempt to worship him would be a very grave sin. He was a human being, and acknowledged publicly that he shared with other humans the ordinary range of human feelings and emotions, joys and limitation of knowledge. He loved, wept, accepted advice. He was an extremely good and noble person – as were all the prophets. He was but one in a long line of Messengers chosen by God.

What do Muslims believe about the Way to God?

The Muslim 'way' to God is called the Shari'ah, from the words '*shari*'', a road, and '*shara'a*', to begin, enter, introduce, prescribe. The Muslim prays to God in every one of the set prayers: 'Show us the straight way, the way of those on whom You have bestowed Your grace, whose portion is not wrath, and who do not go astray.' (Surah 1:6–7). Muslims have been told by Allah: 'This is My straight path, so follow it, and do not follow paths which will separate you from it.' (Surah 6:153; 57:28). The Shari'ah is the code of behaviour for a Muslim. It determines whether any action or detail of life is halal (good and allowed) or *haram* (wrong and forbidden). It involves putting faith in God into action, continually, throughout every aspect of life.

Unlike the Christian 'way', it is not a theological system of belief, although, of course, it is based on the very firm belief that God does exist, along with the whole system of revelation, judgement and life after death. The Christian 'way to God' is to believe certain things about Jesus; and believing in him, to find life in his name. Good deeds are, of course, expected of a Christian; but it is the belief that is paramount. Good deeds can never be enough to earn God's grace or forgiveness – that comes simply as a gift of His compassion.

Muslims also believe that if God punished us according to what we deserved, no living thing would be left on earth![11] To a Muslim, following the shari'ah, that is living out the will of Allah so far as is humanly possible, in whatever circumstances you find yourself, is the only aim that makes sense. One must search for it, and follow it, through all life's tests and temptations, difficulties and tragedies, consciously considering in every situation what the will of God would be for any individual at any given moment.

How do Muslims differ from Christians in their beliefs about Jesus?

The chief difference between a Muslim and a Christian is that Muslims believe that God is the *only* source of blessing and power, and that no human being is divine. Existing things fall into two categories – God, and that-which-is-not-God. God is Creator; everything else is created. A Muslim can never accept pantheism – that God is 'in' nature, or that all nature is 'part of' God – or that a human being (e.g. Jesus, Krishna, Rama *et. al.*) can ever be divine.

To pray for help to any person or thing other than God reveals a lack of true understanding of Him. This division of the unity of God is called in Arabic the sin of *shirk* or 'association'. Jews share this same point of view. The word 'shirk' in the English language means to avoid doing something, usually work. That has nothing whatever to do with the Arabic word, of course.

Muslims do not reject the miraculous nature of Jesus' birth, life, or ascension into Heaven. On the contrary, these beliefs are an important part of their faith; but, unlike Christians, they do not conclude that these prove Jesus to be 'God Incarnate'. To Muslims, God, 'Our Father who is in Heaven', can perform whatever miracles He likes. He has only to say 'Be!' and it is so.[12] The virgin birth of a prophet is indeed a miracle, but it does not make him God. Therefore a Muslim cannot share the Christian point of view as formulated in those creeds of the fourth century AD onwards that strove to account for the humanity of Jesus, who was declared to be 'uncreated', or 'very God of very God, begotten and not made, being of one substance with the Father.' (The Nicene Creed, 325 CE)

This creed, which was formulated after a century of fierce theological argument, did not settle anything. The arguments continued long afterwards, and with the modern debate between Islam and Christianity, it can be seen that those arguments have never really ceased. In fourth-century Alexandria it was taught that the nature of Christ was essentially divine, and that Jesus was God who had *become* a man, his human nature being no more than a 'form'; accordingly Christians could justifiably regard the Virgin Mary as *Theotokos*, or 'Mother of God'. This doctrine was called Monophysite (from 'mono physis' meaning 'one nature'). In Antioch, on the contrary, they emphasised the separateness of the divine and human natures in Jesus, recognising the humanity of Christ as the 'receptacle' of his divinity; therefore he was God *in* a man, and the Virgin Mary was the mother of Jesus as a man, and not of his divine origin; therefore she could certainly *not* be called 'Mother of God'. These were the controversies still rending the Church. The Byzantines became notorious for their cruelty towards the Monophysites, until the coming of the Prophet Muhammad, and the subsequent conversion of vast numbers of Christian Unitarians to Islam.

Is there any evidence in the Christian holy books that the Muslim position concerning Jesus could possibly be right?

Indeed, about 98% of Christian writings actually support the Muslim point of view. Only a tiny part support the Trinitarian view as it was later taught.

The title Jesus preferred for himself was not Son of God, but Son of Man. At the outset of his ministry he was specifically tempted by the Devil to claim that he was Son of God, but three times he resisted, finally rebuffing the Devil with the words: 'Begone, Satan! For it is written "You shall worship the Lord your God, and Him only shall you serve." (Mathew 4:1–10).[13]

Once, a rich young ruler approached Jesus and asked him directly what it was that he had to do in order to attain eternal life. Jesus, surprisingly, if Trinitarians are correct, did not expound to him the 'orthodox' teachings regarding original sin and the need for a redeemer. He said simply: 'Why do you call me good? No one is good but God Alone.' He told him to keep the command-ments, and when the wealthy man commented that he had done so all his life, Jesus requested him to give up his wealth to the poor in exchange for treasure in Heaven. This the man was unable to do, and went away sorrowful. (Mark 10:17–22).

When Jesus taught his disciples to pray, he said '*Our* Father, who art in Heaven.' Yes, Jesus was truly God's dear son – but so are all of us His children.

Indeed, it seems that the earliest strata of the Synoptic Gospels[14], especially the source known as 'Q'[15], did not present Jesus as Son of God in any special sense, but as a *man* regarded by his followers as a prophet, hero and martyr.[16]

If Christians believe that 'no person can come to the Father but by Me (Jesus)', then surely Muslims and Christians can never be reconciled?

A few passages do seem to promote Trinitarian theology, but Muslims feel that Christians should think more deeply about the origin and editing of these passages, as well as their meaning.

The most quoted is probably this one from St John's Gospel: 'I am the way, the truth and the life. No-one comes to the Father, but by me.' (John 14:6).

This is usually taken to mean that a person *must* be a Christian, believing in Jesus as the Son of God, in order to find salvation. The Muslim answer is not to go into scholarly arguments about Gospel-criticism, to deduce which phrases are genuinely from Jesus and which were the work of later editors with axes to grind, but rather to accept that in Jesus' time the phrase was no doubt *true*. Jesus *was* the Messenger of that period. But things changed swiftly, and by six centuries later the original teachings of Christ had been adulterated almost beyond recognition. By the time Muhammad was called to be a Messenger, that particular phrase needed an update!

As for the notion that Jesus was 'one with God' ('I and the Father are one' John 10:39), Muslims suggest that the phrase did not imply the unity of Three Persons in One Godhead, but unity of purpose. 'Holy Father, keep them in Thy name, that they may be one even as we are one...the glory which Thou hast given me I have given to them, that they may be one even as we are one...' (John 17:11,22–24). These sentences were never intended to imply that all believers in God should actually *become part of the Godhead!*

To a Muslim, it is important for Christians to remember that 'eternal life is *this:* 'that they know Thee, the only True God, and Jesus Christ whom Thou hast *sent,'* (John 17:3), 'so that the world may know that Thou hast sent me, and hast loved them even as Thou has loved me.' (John 17:23). 'He who believes in me, believes not in me *but in Him who sent me.'* (John 12:44).

What do Muslims teach about personal salvation?

The most important aspect of how an individual achieves personal salvation is *taqwa,* or God-consciousness. Once the realisation that God is Real has dawned on a person, their life can never be the same again. Life now takes on a whole new perspective. It is no longer just a matter of waking up in the morning, going through the day's work and pleasures (or sufferings), and then sleeping again until one finally passes into oblivion. Suddenly, there is perspective to it all, a purpose, an aim. There is a spiritual dimension, and it is more important than the mere physical. There is a sense of justice and fulfilment, and also a strong feeling of relationship with a Power that is not only Supreme, but also Good, who cares very much for humanity and is deeply involved with every action and thought of our lives.

People who have no God-consciousness cannot understand the joy, the devotion, the urge to serve, that goes along with it. This awareness might be granted suddenly to a person, in a flash of insight, or it might come only after a long struggle and search. It can only come very late to a person who is really in a state of sleep – who never thinks about the questions 'who am I?', 'why am I here?', 'what is my life for?' and 'where am I going?'

The Prophet Muhammad taught that if a person wished to start on the road of belief, they should perhaps try living *as if* they believed, as if they could accept that God was aware of everything about them. 'He sees you,' said the Prophet, 'even if you cannot see Him.' This living leads to awareness, and is known as *ihsan*.

Belief is the key to the way of life, but there are two aspects to it. Firstly, one must develop religious devotion in practices such as prayer; secondly, in the everyday manner in which one strives to please God by putting the principles of faith into practice. Belief in God makes a person aim high and try to live in the best possible way. This effort is known as the *Greater Jihad*. [17] The two concepts are known in Islam as *iman* (faith) and *amal* (action). Belief in God is not enough. A Muslim's life has to show some transformation because of that belief. Many people may pray at great length and forgo all personal pleasures, but remain selfish and cruel. Islam teaches that in this case, such faith is really only skin-deep. If their hearts are not changed all they will gain is sleeplessness, hunger and discomfort, coupled with a self-deceiving pride.

Belief in God on its own does not make a person Muslim. No-one had greater belief in God than Shaytan, but he used his free will to oppose God's will, not to submit to it. Maybe he even thought he 'knew better' than God. Many religious people do. As Jesus' brother James put it in his New Testament epistle: 'You believe that God is One? You do well. Even the demons believe, and shudder.' (James 2:19).

On the other hand, one's good deeds are not enough. According to the Prophet: 'there is no person whose deeds alone can secure salvation for him/her.' They asked: 'Allah's Messenger, not even you?' Whereupon he said: 'Not even I, but that the mercy of Allah takes hold of me.' (Muslim). The two aspects must go together, and support each other. Belief without good works and life is meaningless, as is the good life without belief. Quoting James again – 'You have your faith and I have my works. Show me your faith apart from your works, and I by my works will show you my faith… Do you need to be shown, you foolish fellow, that faith apart from works is barren?...As the body apart from the spirit is dead, so faith apart from works is dead.' (James 2:18–26).

Islam not only acclaims good works, but regards them as that which justifies people in the sight of God, Who warns us that not one iota of good work or of evil doings will be missed on the Day of

Reckoning, but will, on the contrary, form the basis of our judgement, subject only to His mercy.

Non-Muslims also have the record of their works done to justify themselves in Muslim eyes, and establish themselves as people of piety and saintliness. In Islam, works earn merit with God, regardless of the religious faith of those who do them.

What does Islam teach about forgiveness?

There is no such thing as a perfect person. We all have numerous shortcomings, are sometimes blind to our faults and sins, and are frequently weak in the face of temptation. On our journey from childhood to adult life, we commit so many sins, or fail to do so many things we ought to do, that the situation may appear almost hopeless. How can we possibly put right all the things we have done wrong?

Thanks be to God for His great mercy. Thanks to His compassion, the moment a person is truly sorry, he or she is forgiven. Allah stated clearly to the Prophet this message:

> *'O My servants, who have transgressed against their souls. Do not despair of the mercy of God, for He forgives all sins, He is Oft-Forgiving, Most Merciful.'* (Surah 39:53).

Once, the Prophet reported that the Devil said: 'By my honour, O Lord, I shall never stop misguiding Your servants so long as life remains in their bodies!' The Almighty, the Glorious Lord, said: 'By My honour, I shall never cease forgiving them, so long as they ask forgiveness of Me!' (Ahmad).

Another wonderful saying is: 'O son of Adam – so long as you call upon Me and ask of Me, I shall forgive you for what you have done, and I shall not mind. O son of Adam, were your sins to reach the clouds of the sky and were you then to ask forgiveness of Me, I would forgive you. O son of Adam, were you to come to Me with sins as great as the earth itself, and were you then to face Me ascribing no partner to Me, I would bring you forgiveness in equal measure.' (Tirmidhi, Ahmad).

What wonderful mercy – how gracious, and how undeserved!

However, it has to be said that just as some humans refuse to stop on the crazy path to their own doom, despite the intercession of their loved ones, so the future lives of some people will be unpleasant because of their absolute refusal to accept the love and mercy of God and to live in a way acceptable to Him.

'If God were to punish people according to their wrongdoing, He would not leave on earth a single living creature; but He gives them respite for a stated term; and when their term expires, they will not be able to delay (their fate) for a single hour, just as they cannot bring it forward by a single hour.' (Surah 16:61).

One's personal salvation lies in one's own hands, and in the supreme compassion of Allah, who loves each individual He has created.

What do Muslims think Jesus taught about personal salvation?

They think he taught what Islam teaches, what Allah revealed. Muslims would base their reasoning on the divine compassion and love of God, who always forgives people who turn to Him, so long as their repentance is genuine. The eternal fate of that soul is then in the hands of God, who alone can reward or condemn for ever, or can forgive, as He wills.

Jesus taught this very clearly in the famous parable of the Prodigal Son. A foolish young man sinned, and ended up in the gutter. When he came to his senses and realised what he had done he decided to go home and beg for forgiveness – perhaps his father would take him back as a servant. The father (who represents God in this story) saw him while he was still a long way off and ran out to welcome him back. 'This my son was dead,' he said, 'but now he is alive again. He was lost, and is found.' (Luke 15:11–32).

Islam (like all the Jewish prophets) teaches that it is nonsense to think that any sacrifice of blood, animal or human, can somehow bribe God, or 'buy' God's forgiveness; it is only the turning of the heart that can do that. We can never really adequately earn God's forgiveness, but we have been taught that what matters is our love for Him, and how we live, how hard we try.

Jesus taught, in the parable of the Sheep and the Goats (Mathew 25:31–46) that a person's entry into the Kingdom of Heaven was not based so much on their religious faith, knowledge or intelligence (for they might be simple souls indeed) but on whether they fed the hungry, clothed the naked, visited the sick, and so forth.

Very similar messages were given to the Prophet Muhammad in many of the hadiths:

> *Allah said: 'I am near to the thoughts of My servants when they think about Me, and I am with them when they remember Me... If anyone draws the length of a hand's span nearer to Me, I shall draw the length of a cubit nearer towards him... If anyone comes to Me walking, I shall come to him at the run. And if anyone meets Me with sins the size of earth, but has not associated anything with Me, I shall forgive him.' (Muslim).*

> *'On the Day of Judgement Allah will say: 'O son of Adam, I fell ill and you did not visit Me.' The man will answer, 'O Lord, how could I have visited You when You are Lord of the worlds?' He will say:'Did you not know that My servant had fallen ill, and you did not visit him? Truly, if you had visited him, you would have found Me with him.'* (Hadith Qudsi).

Faith by itself, no matter how devout, is not enough. The Devil is a great believer in God! Very devout people can be misguided and spend their lives believing the wrong things. True belief is always backed up by the quality of a person's life. This was also the message taught by Jesus' brother James, his successor and the first leader of the Church of Jerusalem.

'What does it profit, my brothers, if a person says he has faith, but has not works? Can his faith save him?

If a brother or sister is ill-clad and in need of food, and one of you says: 'Go in peace, be warm and be full' without giving them the things needed, what does it profit? Faith by itself, if it has no works, is dead...I, by my works, will show you my faith.' (James 2:14–18).

If Muhammad was really a genuine prophet, why was he not foretold in the Bible as Jesus was?

Most Muslims do not have the necessary scholarship to answer this fairly. In fact, some with Biblical knowledge *have* seen possible prophecies in the Old Testament, even though it is fair to point out that other prophets, such as Moses or Isaiah, were not foretold. There is no particular reason why Muhammad should have been. Being foretold was not a necessary attribute of a prophet. [18]

It has been suggested that in the New Testament, Mathew 11:11 is a possible prophecy. Jesus said: 'Truly I say to you, among those born of women there has risen no-one greater than John the Baptist; yet he who is least in the Kingdom of Heaven is greater than he.' It is a hard saying, and the most charitable meaning Christians have proposed is that since John the Baptist did not accept Jesus as the 'one who was to come', all Christians who did had progressed further than he. A Muslim suggestion is that the word *least* (saghir) really meant the *last* of the Prophets sent by Allah – the word saghir often being used in Arabic for the youngest of a family. Muslims would put greater emphasis on the words of Jn 1: 21 and 25 – the Jews sent priests and Levites from Jerusalem to ask John the Baptist (the son of one of their own number, Zechariah the priest): 'Who are you? (Are you the Christ?, this part of the question implied). Are you Elijah? Are you the prophet?' John answered in the negative to all three suggestions, but notice that there were *three* suggestions. They further asked him: 'Then why are you baptizing, if you are neither the Christ, nor Elijah, nor the prophet?' This has always puzzled Christians because they have not been made familiar with the fact that *another* prophet was expected who was separate from the Christ.

Let us take another New Testament reference, that of the long Farewell Discourse given by Jesus on the night of his last supper, compiled in chapters 14–17 of St John's Gospel. In these verses, Jesus refers several times to the coming of the Holy Spirit, the Paraclete or Advocate. Muslims suggest that these are really references to the coming of the Prophet Muhammad. They do not accept that the Holy Spirit is a separate 'person' in a Holy Trinity, but that it is the action of God which has always existed, just as God has always existed. They regard as unacceptable and extremely odd the notion that the Holy Spirit was not active while Jesus lived on earth, or that he had to return to the Father in order for it to descend and start working again and are perplexed when they are expected to accept that this is what Jesus believed. Yet in these passages the Holy Spirit really does seem to refer to a person.

Let us briefly look at the references:

'The Paraclete, the Holy Spirit, whom the Father will send in my name, he will teach you all things and bring (back) to your remembrance all that I have said to you (John 14:26)...When the Paraclete comes, whom I shall send to you from the Father, even the spirit of truth who proceeds from the Father, he will bear witness to me (John 15:26)... He will convince the world of sin and of righteousness and of judgement (John 16:8)... He will guide you into all the truth; for he will not speak on his own authority, but whatever he hears he will speak, and he will declare to you the things which are to come. He will glorify me, for he will take what is mine and declare it to you (John 16:13–15).

To a Muslim this seems to prophecy very strikingly the calling of the Prophet Muhammad. Of course, no Muslim is trying to claim that Muhammad is the third person in the Holy Trinity, as some outraged Christians might think. However, there is very interesting speculation that the Greek word 'parakletos' – which is a legal term for an advocate or counsel for the defence – might refer to the role of the Prophet Muhammad in defending the true beliefs of Jesus against the Trinitarian overgrowths; or, more interestingly, that the word is a corruption of 'periklytos' – which means 'the Praised One'. Non-Muslims, and any who do not speak Arabic, will be unaware that the name Muhammad means 'the praised one', from the root 'hamd' (praise or glory).

If Muslims are supposed to accept that all the Jewish prophets were genuine, why do they not have the same reverence for the Old Testament that Jews and Christians have?

Most ordinary Muslims are not scholars and are probably unfamiliar with the Bible. However, these days most Christians have not read it either; moreover, up to a few hundred years ago, it could only be read by those who spoke Greek, Hebrew or Latin, and for a long time the Church fought fiercely to prevent it from being translated into the languages ordinary people spoke. This was because theologians anticipated all the difficulties that would arise over interpretations, and wished to keep these controversies in the hands of scholarly priests, and away from questioning laymen who might begin to exercise their own reason and intellect upon the texts.

Muslim scholars *do* respect the Bible, but the passages we have already briefly looked at probably indicate to the alert reader that they can only revere the Jewish or Christian texts with certain provisos. Where a clear teaching is 'the Word of the Lord' revealed by a prophet, these seem to be completely in keeping with what was revealed later to Muhammad (Allah's peace and blessings be upon him). However, Muslim scholars concur with many modern Christian academics that much of the Old and New Testament was not directly reported from God, but was the work of very human authors and editors, who included, omitted or altered material in accordance with their own principles. Therefore, it is 'open season' for any theologians to make their own informed decisions as to whether or not a particular passage, recorded saying or miracle, is accurately reported.

Most Christian scholars would not find themselves very far from the Islamic position, although it is unlikely that either Muslim or Christian 'people-in-the street' would be able to follow the controversies fully, unless they had studied theology. No doubt a committed Trinitarian Christian would argue that such a very Jewish phrase as the one about Christians being obliged to keep the entire Jewish Law with no changes, not even so much as a jot or a tittle (Mt 5:17–19) was not a genuine saying of Jesus but the invention of a very pro-Jewish gospel editor, possibly a converted Jewish scribe, and therefore could be rejected. But these Trinitarians find it hard to accept that Muslims reject the very few Trinitarian references to Jesus being Son of God in the Christian 'orthodox' sense, as also the work of an editor.

One thing that should satisfy Muslims is the absence *shirk anywhere* in the Old Testament. Up until the time of Jesus, no Jewish teacher or prophet was *ever* revealed, or even given to suspect the notion that God was really Three Persons in One, or that an Original Sin had been committed by Adam for which all future human beings were to be punished until God would incarnate Himself as a means of redeeming their souls. Indeed, the entire campaign of the Old Testament prophets was to maintain the *unity* of God against the many Baal cults of the region, that *were* trinitarian, and *did* have virgin-born, dying-and rising saviour gods. [19]

The prophets also taught that God's true 'nation' was not a particular race of people, but a 'nation' of those who believed and accepted certain divine Laws as guidance and shaped their lives according to certain religious and charitable principles.

What alarms Muslims is that there is a sinister thread in the Old Testament that teaches something quite different – that the Jewish people *were* a special race, and that when certain of the Old Testament writers (and certain of the modern politically active Jews) looked back upon their history, they invoked that notion while slaughtering their enemies or extending their territories, claiming that they were commanded by God to do so.

Colonialists of all epochs and all nations have always sought a justification for their annexations, looting and pillaging. Everything is permitted if one is 'God's chosen people', doing 'God's will'. The Crusaders considered themselves the 'arm of God', as did the Inquisitors, the Quaker settlers who initiated the genocide of the Native American, those settlers who tried to wipe out the Australian Aborigine, the 'holy Russians' of the pogroms, the 'Gott mit uns' in the Germany of Bismarck, Hitler with Auschwitz, the 'Christ's soldiers' sent from

America to Vietnam, or the 'people of God entrusted with a mission' in Vorster's South Africa.

In fact, the idea of the Jews as a chosen race is historically infantile, for those who would call themselves Jews hail from virtually every race on earth. Also, it is worth pointing out that because all expansionist groups have expressed this privileged conception of themselves, why should the writings of one people alone be accepted? Furthermore, such a claim always sanctifies aggression, expansion and domination; also it is theologically intolerable, for if some are 'chosen' it means that the others are 'rejected' and beyond hope – hardly the sublime message of spiritualism as taught by the prophets.

The tendency to blind fanaticism and hard-heartedness is not, of course, confined in any way to Jewish history, but it is fair to comment that the prophets of the Old Testament were well aware of this tendency among their people, and spoke out against it frequently, often with fatal consequences for themselves. Jesus, for example, said: 'O Jerusalem, Jerusalem – killing the prophets and stoning those who are sent to you! How often would I have gathered your children together as a hen gathers her brood under her wings, but you would not! Behold, your house is forsaken and desolate. I tell you, you will not see me again until you say 'Blessed is he who comes in the name of the Lord.' (Mt 23:37–39)

So far as the wonderful teachings of the Messenger Jesus in the New Testament are concerned, Muslims believe they have been adulterated by the doctrine of the Holy Trinity – a doctrine that they claim Jesus never taught. They believe that the original Church (led by St James from Jerusalem in conjunction with the mission-work of St Peter) did not envisage a break with Judaism at all.

'Think not that I have come to abolish the Law and the prophets; I have not come to abolish them, but to fulfil them. Truly I say to you, till heaven and earth pass away, not a jot[20] nor a tittle[21] will pass from the law until all is accomplished. Whoever, then, relaxes one of the least of these commandments and teaches people so, shall be called least in the Kingdom of Heaven.' (Mt 5:17–19).

However, the Trinitarian theology becomes necessary for the salvation of humanity if one accepts the belief in transmitted Original Sin, the hopeless condition of humanity, and the fear that God is not able for some reason to forgive His repentant 'prodigal sons' without becoming incarnate and sacrificing Himself.

It is a great pity that more Christians do not study the developing thought of the Old Testament more closely – especially the highly significant passage of Ezekiel 18 (particularly 1–4,14–17, 20–23, 30–31) only 'the soul that sins shall die. The son *shall not suffer for the iniquity of the father*' etc.

Here, it clearly demonstrates how erroneous is the old notion that the sins of the ancestors were able to influence the eternal fate of the living. God judges each individual on his or her own merits. Once we accept Ezekiel 18 as a true revelation the whole message of atonement theology becomes unnecessary.

Do Muslims believe in miracles?

Yes. Miracles are regarded as acts of God that somehow break or intrude on the laws of nature in order to bring about some amazing event. Pious people tend to have a strong belief in miracles on the grounds that Allah can do as He wishes and may intervene and disturb the laws of nature as He wills.

It is not God's way to compel humans to believe anything; the idea of confronting a human with a miracle in order to have him or her believe is not how God normally works. We are always given the freedom to choose between right and wrong. When certain nonbelievers tried to get the Prophet Muhammad to perform various miracles so as to enable them to believe in his message, the request was always refused. 'Say: My Lord is high above these things. I am only a man, and His Messenger.' (Surah 17:90–93). In fact, miracles much greater than their foolish whims were already before them. The revelation of the Qur'an in itself being the greatest miracle.

Christians will note that Jesus also encountered this issue. One of the temptations he faced at the start of his ministry was to prove that he was the Son of God by jumping off the pinnacle on the Temple in Jerusalem, a drop of many hundreds of feet to the rocks below. God would certainly save him from harm (Mt 4:5–7; Lk 4:9–12). Jesus' answer to Satan was that 'you shall not put your Lord to the test!' – a quotation from Deuteronomy 6:16 – God's words to Moses.

Although the Prophet Jesus is the one celebrated in Islam for being the 'miracle-worker' by the will of God, the Prophet Muhammad was also believed to have worked some miracles, but this is not stressed. He never claimed to be superhuman, or to have supernatural abilities. He was asked to say in the Qur'an that: 'I have no control over what may be helpful to me or hurtful to me, but as Allah wills. Had I the full knowledge of the Unseen, I should increase my good, and evil should not touch me. (But) I am only a warner, an announcer of good tidings to those who believe.' (Surah 7:188).

My mother's question – why did my daughter, who I have always believed to be intelligent and in her right mind, choose to become one of these Muslims?

Dear reader, I hope that if you have read my book through, I do not need to add anything to what I have already said. Like so many other people who have converted to Islam, I have found that it answers so many of the things I used to question, whether in the realm of theology or morality and ethics. I have shared with so many other converts, the feeling of finding my place at last, of coming home.

I cannot claim to be a good Muslim – God knows I do so many things wrong, and make so many mistakes. Thank God, that He does not punish us according to what we really deserve, but is the wonderful Compassionate and Merciful One. A true Muslim cannot claim to be a perfect person – that is ridiculous. Human beings are full of faults, give in to temptations, blunder into situations where they are well out of their depth, say things they do not really mean, run away from unpleasant situations and issues, turn a blind eye to things they feel they cannot cope with. We all do it, even though we may try hard to be good servants of God. We all know the arrogance of those who *think* that they are perfect – or at least, that they are a good deal nearer the mark than you are – and I suppose we can be smugly content that these sorts usually drive people *away* from God rather than bringing the hopeless a little nearer to Him. It is not for us to judge anyone, thank God. That is for Him, and Him alone – and what He looks for is not only our deeds, but also our motivations and intentions.

I was a head of RE in a state school for over thirty years, and had to write thousands of reports on struggling students, as well as brilliant ones. How often I came across the intelligent pupil who was 'A' for academic ability, but as regards character, I would not give more than an 'E', if there was such a slot on the report-form. Vice versa, how often I came across pupils with the brain-power of a caterpillar, but who were wonderful people, warm-hearted, modest, hard-working, unselfish and kind. Thank God, He is not going to test us and judge us on our brains – they are not our responsibility, for He Himself doled them out to us. There are no nasty exams which brand us as failures and make us look stupid. No, what is important is what we *do* with our lives, how we dedicate them to the service of others, and try to leave our particular patch in the world a little better than we found it, if possible.

I also believe that one of the most important qualities in any person is *honesty*, integrity in one's personal life, and also in following what one believes to be true. It is for that reason, therefore, that I chose to become 'one of those Muslims' – not because I suddenly didn't like Jesus any more, or that I suddenly became 'political' and wanted to become a terrorist, or that I suddenly decided I must be completely subservient to some man or other. These things have nothing to do with Islam. I became Muslim because I was, in a small way, a theologian – and because when I discovered the real teachings of Islam, I believed them to be right. I didn't want to cause trouble, or upset my family, or offend anybody – but there came a time when I was in a

Church service of Holy Communion, and I realised that I simply could no longer stand up and recite the Christian creed with any conviction.

I rarely discuss theology with my parents. It embarrasses and irritates them. My mother staunchly resists any notion of being 'taken over', and is pacified when I point out that the Qur'an advises us to leave others alone, apart from setting our examples as best we can, providing answers when asked, and preaching what we believe when called upon to do so, or whenever we have a suitable opportunity. Surah 109 reads:

> *'Say: O you who do not believe, I do not worship that which you worship, and you will not worship that which I worship. And I will not worship that which you have always been used to worship, nor will you worship what I worship. To you be your way, and to me be mine.'*

To each person is the responsibility for what they believe. Belief cannot be forced, it can only be offered to others with the reasons for it. People with ideas and beliefs of their own usually regard as annoying pests those who come along full of missionary zeal. They do not appreciate having someone else's fervour rammed down their throats. Nevertheless, I have done my best to come up with a few explanations, and answer some of the questions I have heard most often from critics of Islam. I honestly believe that these criticisms are almost always based on wrong information about Islam, and once it has been explained properly, and some clear blue water inserted between the activities of the extreme 'left and right wings' of Islam, insha'Allah, many more will be drawn towards what we Muslims regard as the Straight Path.

So, I pray that God will richly bless all you readers of this book, and bring you to peace and understanding of His great love and compassion. Amen.

Notes

1. Exodus 3:14.
2. This topic is covered in depth by Ismail Raji al-Faruqi, *Islam and other Faiths*, Leicester: The Islamic Foundation, 1998, pp.75, et al.
3. al-Faruqi, op. cit., pp87–88.
4. Bible scholars will be very familiar with such 'editors' as J, E, D and P, (ie. Yahwistic, Elohist, Deuteronomic and Priestly), and other details of source and form criticism.
5. All those interested in the history of Unitarianism, and the general history of the Trinitarian dogmas and controversies concerning them, should read these two books: *Jesus, Prophet of Islam* (revised edition) by Muhammad 'Ata-ur-Rahman and Ahmad Thomson, London: Ta-Ha Publications, 1996, and *Christianity in the Arab World* by al-Hassan bin Talal of Jordan, London: SCM Press, 1998.
6. *Jesus, Prophet of Islam*, p.157.
7. It was said that few of his companions could read or write. Those who could included both men and women; the women included his wives Aishah bint Abu Bakr, Hafsah bint Umar, Umm Salamah bint Abu Umayyah and Zaynab bint Jahsh.

8. Jesus had a similar problem in his supposed home-town of Nazareth, where he was rejected by those who had known him all his life, and commented that 'a prophet is not without honour, except in his own country and amongst his own people'.
9. For example, in the narrative of the Prophet Abraham sacrificing his son, it is the son Ishmael and not Isaac, according to the Qur'an.
10. A surah (meaning 'a step up') is a chapter in the Qur'an. The word for one verse is an *ayah* (meaning 'a sign').
11. Surah 16:61.
12. Surah 3:47.
13. Christian commentaries usually interpret the temptations of Jesus in a completely different way He was tempted to turn stones to bread, to jump off the pinnacle of the Temple, and to bow down and worship the devil in order to be given all the kingdoms of the world. A careful reading of the words reveals that what Jesus was really being tempted to do was to say and believe that he was the Son of God, which he absolutely refused to do.
14. The three gospels named after Matthew, Mark and Luke are called 'Synoptic' because their accounts of the events in the life of Jesus follow more or less the same synopsis or outline.
15. The name 'Q' comes simply from the German word 'quelle', meaning 'a source'. By definition it consists of the verses common to Matthew and Luke which are not in Mark.
16. See, for example, Luke 4:19, 24; 7:16; 8:33, where Jesus is called a prophet; Luke 3:13, 26; 4:27, 30, where Jesus is called a servant of God; Acts 2:22, where Peter calls Jesus a 'man approved of God'; and I Timothy 2:5 where Paul says 'There is One God, and one mediator between God and humanity, the *man* Jesus Christ.'
17. The word 'jihad' comes from the Arabic word 'to strive' or 'to struggle'.

18. Some suggested passages include Deuteronomy 33:1–3; Isaiah 21:40; 42:1–21; Habakkuk 3:3.
19. My forthcoming book 'Mysteries of Jesus' provides evidence that all the doctrines and rituals of Trinitarian Christianity were in place long before the earthly life of Jesus, and might have existed until this century had Jesus never been born at all!
20. A *jot* (or yod) was the smallest letter in the Hebrew alphabet.
21. A tittle was a scribal flourish on an individual letter, which could alter the entire meaning of the word. For example, in Hebrew the letters 'g' and 'r' are identical but for a tittle. If you take the word 'gimel' which means camel, and omit the tittle at the bottom of the 'g', the word becomes 'rimel' which means rope. Therefore, we have the famous example of Jesus' saying 'it is easier for a camel to go through the eye of a needle than for a rich man to enter the Kingdom of Heaven.' One Gospel version, the Codex Bezae, has 'rope' instead of 'camel'.

Index

A
Aaron/Harun, 23
'Abdul Hamid, 94
Abortions, 70
Abraham/Ibrahim, 4, 23, 54, 55, 56, 73, 104, 105, 115, 116
Abu Bakr, 61, 74, 83
Abu Sufyan, 98
Abu Talib, 61
Adam, 23, 54, 56, 128, 135
Aelia Capitolina, 89,
Afterlife/Akhirah, 28, 32, 33
Ahmad, 128
'Aishah, 61, 73, 74,
Akhirah *see* Afterlife
Alexandria, 121
'Ali, 61, 62
'Amal, 125
Amos, 4
Angels, 16, 17, 18, 19, 101
Anglican(s), 1
Antioch, 121
Al-Aqsa Mosque, 89
Arabic, 13, 94, 104, 120, 133
Arabs, 80, 89, 93
Arafat, Yasser, 90
Arafat, 54
Archbishop of Canterbury, 112
Armenia, 88
Ashrawi, Hanan, 90
'Asr, 45
Auschwitz, 136
Australian Aborigine, 136
Ayatollah(s), 47, 48
'Azrail, 19

B
Baalism, 103
Badr, 74

Baghdad, 87, 88
Balkh, 87
Bangladeshis, 93
Banking system, 86
Barakah, 37
Barzakh, 29
Baybars, 88
Bethleham, 5
Bible, the, 8, 17, 22, 23, 54, 131, 134
Biblical scholars, 98, 103; texts: 6, 8
Bilhah, 73
Bismarck, 136
Black Stone, 57
Borgia Popes, 3
Britain, 1
Buddhism, 32
Buddhists, 111
Bukhara, 87
Burial customs, 7
Byzantine, 121

C

China, 94
Christian Unitarians (see Unitarians), 111, 121
Christian(s), 3, 4, 5, 6, 11, 15, 16, 17, 22, 25, 27, 29, 38, 44, 47, 49, 73, 81, 82, 83, 88, 89, 90, 97, 98,102, 103, 104, 106, 107, 108, 109, 110, 115, 116, 117, 118, 119, 123, 124, 131, 132, 133, 134, 135, 140
Christianity, 2, 3, 4, 12, 71, 82, 90, 102, 104, 105, 106, 109, 112, 121
Christmas, 5, 81, 82
Church, 7, 8, 107, 111, 112, 113, 134, 138, 143
Church of England, 111, 112
Church of Jerusalem, 130
Circumcision, 71
Classical Arguments, 10
Companions, 21
Comparative religion, 2
Concubines, 73
Crusaders, 136
Crusades, 1, 102

D

Dar al-Dawah, 93
Dar al-Harb, 93
Dar al-Islam, 91
David/Dawud, 22, 23, 73, 104, 105
Deuteronomy, 34,100, 140

Dhikr, 12, 35, 36, 38
Dhu al-Hijja, 53
Divorce, 75, 76, 78
Dowry, 79
Du'a, 43, 44

E

Easter, 5
Egypt, 71, 72
Elijah, 23
Elijah/Ilyas, 23, 132
Elisha/al-Yas'a, 23
Enoch/Idris, 23
Europe, 1, 84
European Trinitarian Christian, 113
Eve/Hawwah, 54
Ezekiel, 4, 23, 138, 139

F

Fajr, 45
Falah, 34
Farewell Sermon, 80
Fatalism, 25
Fatimah, 48, 61, 62
Free will, 25, 26
Fundamentalists, 65

G

Gabriel, 19, 55, 114
Germany, 89, 136
Ghadir Khumm 61
al-Ghayb, 27, 60
Ghenghis Khan, 87
Ghusl, 44
Gospel(s), 22, 122, 123, 132
Greek, 134

H

Habash, George, 90
Hadith, 114, 130
Hafiz, 21, 114
Hafsah, 21, 114
Hagar/Hajir, 54, 55, 73
Hajj see Pilgrimage
Halal, 118
Halal slaughter, 84
Hamd, 37
Hammas, 90
Haram, 118
Heaven/*Jannah,* 29, 30, 31, 33, 35, 38, 57, 102, 107, 120, 122, 129
Hebrew, 103, 134
Hell/*Jahannum,* 29, 30, 31, 32, 33, 34, 35
High Anglican, 111

Hijri, 53
Hinduism, 32
Hitler, 136
Holy Communion, 47, 143
Holy Spirit, 17, 132, 133
Hosea, 4
Hud, 23
Hulagu, 87, 88

I

Ibn al-Arabi, 11
Id ul-Adha, 54, 55
Ihram, 53
Ihsan, 125
Imam, 48, 62
Iman, 6, 125
India, 94
Indonesia(ns), 93, 94
Inquisition, 3
Inquisitors, 136
Iran(ians), 61, 93
Iraq, 61
Isaac/Ishaq, 23, 55, 116
Isaiah, 4, 16, 131
'Isha 45, 52
Ishmael/Ismail, 23, 54, 55, 56, 116
Islamic state, 63, 105, 106
Israel, 88, 89, 94, 108
Israfil, 19
Istanbul, 22
Itikaf, 52

J

Jacob/Yaqub, 23, 73, 116
Jamarat, 54
St.James, 107, 126, 130, 131, 138
Jehovah, 102
Jehovah's Witnesses, 82
Jeremiah, 4, 16
Jerusalem, 89, 132, 137, 138, 140
Jesus Christ/Isa, 3, 5, 16, 22, 23, 24, 27, 32, 33, 34, 38, 47, 64, 81, 82, 83, 84, 99, 100, 103, 104, 105, 106, 107, 108, 109, 113, 115, 116, 117, 119, 120, 121, 122, 123, 124,126, 129, 130, 131, 132, 133, 135, 137, 138, 140, 142
Jethro, 23
Jew(s), 3, 4, 83, 88, 94, 98, 100, 104, 105, 106, 107, 109, 110, 112, 120, 132, 134, 136, 137

Jewish, 6, 49, 84, 80, 90, 99, 115, 129, 135
Jihad, 63, 125
Jinn, 20
Job/Ayyub, 23
St. John, 64, 123, 124, 131, 132, 133
John the Baptist/Yahya, 4, 24, 104, 131, 132
Jonah/Yunus, 24
Joseph/Yusuf, 23, 105
Joshua, 108
Judaic, 108
Judaism, 104, 105, 109, 138
Judgement, 30, 31, 127
Judgement (Day of), 6, 19, 30, 38, 99, 127, 130
Jupiter, 89

K
Ka'bah, 53, 54, 55, 56, 57, 98
Karbela, 61
Kemal, Mustafa, 94
Keturah, 73
Krishna, 120

L
Latin, 134
Laylat al-Qadr, 52
Leah, 73
Levites, 132
Life after death, 107
Life to come, 39

M
Madinah, 46, 95, 101
Maghrib, 45,
Makkah, 52, 56, 81, 101
Malaysians, 93
Mameluke, 88
Marwa, 54
Mass, 47
Mesopotamia, 105
Middle East, 90, 104, 107
Mikail, 19
Miracles, 120
Mishnah, 6
Mongol, 87, 88
Monophysite, 121
Moorish conquerors, 102
Moses/Musa, 4, 22, 23, 83, 103, 104, 115, 131, 140
Mosque(s), 45, 67
Muhammad, the Prophet, 6, 15, 20, 24, 27, 37, 46, 54, 56, 64, 73, 83, 97, 101, 104, 105, 113, 114, 116, 117, 118, 121, 123, 125, 130, 131, 132133, 134, 139, 140
Mujtahid, 47
Mullah, 47

Munkir, 19
Muslim calendar, 50
Muslim children, 68
Muslim countries, 3
Muslim scholars, 4
Muslim statement of faith, 6

N

Najran, 106
Nakir, 19
New age religion, 17
New Testament, 16, 22, 103, 131, 132, 134, 138
Nicene Creed, 120
Nisab, 49
Noah/Nuh, 23, 104

O

Old Testament, 17, 34, 103, 107, 134, 135, 136, 137, 138
Original Sin, 135, 138

P

Pakistan(is), 93, 94
Palestine, 89
Palestinians, 88, 89, 90
Pan-Arabism, 93, 94
Paraclete, 133
Paradise, 33, 34
Parents, 2
St.Paul, 107, 108, 109
People of the Book, 104
Peter, 84
Pilgrimage/*Hajj,* 43, 52, 53, 54, 57, 81, 101
PLO (Palestine Liberation Organisation), 88, 90
Polygamy, 38, 39, 73
Prayer/Salah, 43, 44, 101, 115
Protestants, 112
Psalm, 16

Q

Qadi, 47
al-Qadr, 24
Qiblah, 55, 56, 57
Qom, 61
Quaker, 111, 136
Quran, the, 15, 17, 19, 20, 21, 22, 23, 24, 26, 30, 39, 51, 52, 54, 57, 71, 73, 77, 80, 98, 104, 113, 114, 115, 116, 117, 139, 143

R

Rabbi Hillel, 100
Rachel, 73
Racism, 64

Rama, 120
Ramadan, 49, 50, 51, 53, 101
Reckoning (Day of) (See Judgement), 127
Riba, 86, 87
Roman Catholic(ism) (Church), 3, 47, 111, 112
Romans, 89
RSPCA, 85

S

Sabr, 28
Sadaqah, 49
Safa, 54
Sa'i, 55
Salih, 23
Salvation Army, 111
Samarkand, 87
Sarah, 55, 73
Satan/Shaytan, 20, 126
Sawm, 43, 50
Seveners, 48
Shahadah, 43, 97, 98
Shahid, 64
Shammai, 100
Shari'ah, 75, 118
Shi'ite, 48, 60
Shirk, 82, 120
Shuayb, 23
Solomon/Sulayman, 4, 22, 23, 68, 73, 89, 104
Somalia, 71
Sophronius, 89
South Africa, 137
Spain, 102
St. Thomas Aquinas, 10
State school(s), 2
Sudan, 71
Sunnah, 60, 61, 62
Sunni, 60, 61, 62
Sun-worship, 45

T

Talmud, the, 6
Taqwa, 52, 124
Tarawih, 52
Tashkent, 21
Tawaf, 54
Tawhid, 6, 14
Temple, 89, 140
Terrorism, 64
Terrorists (IRA), 3
Timur the Lame, 87
Tirmidhi, 128
Torah, the, 16, 35, 105, 106
Trinitarian(ism), 5, 16, 82, 113, 117, 121, 123, 135, 136, 138
Trinity, 111, 112, 132, 133, 138
Twelvers, 48

U

Ubayy ibn Ka'b, 115
UK (United Kingdom), 1, 2, 68, 70, 85, 111, 112
'Umar, 21, 61, 89
Umm Atiyyah, 71
Ummah, 45
Umrah, 53
Unitarians (see Christian Unitarians), 111, 112, 113
USA (United States of America), 84, 93, 94, 137
'Uthman, 61

V

Vietnam, 137
Virgin Mary/Maryam, 56, 121
Vorster, 137

W

Women (Muslim), 46, 53, 66, 77
Wudu, 44

Y

Yahweh, 102, 103

Z

Zakah, 43, 49, 50, 101
Zakat-ul-fitr, 50
Zamzam, 55
Zechariah/Zakariyyah, 24, 132
Zilpah, 73
Zionism, 89
Zionist movement, 88
Zuhur, 45

Printed in Spain

Liberdúplex Artes Gráficas

Tel.: 00 34 609 54 07 01
Fax: 00 34 937 53 09 87